DATE DUE

*Financing Public Elementary
and Secondary Education*

THE LIBRARY OF EDUCATION

A Project of The Center for Applied Research in Education, Inc.

G. R. Gottschalk, Director

Advisory Board:

Ralph W. Tyler, Chairman
James E. Allen, Jr.
C. Ray Carpenter
Harold C. Case
Theodore A. Distler
Henry H. Hill
Monsignor Frederick G. Hochwalt
Paul A. Miller
Harold G. Shane
Harold Spears

Editorial Board:

Walter A. Anderson, Chairman
John S. Brubacher
Morey R. Fields
Eric F. Gardner
Daniel E. Griffiths
John Dale Russell

Categories of Coverage

I	II	III
Curriculum and Teaching	Administration, Organization, and Finance	Psychology for Educators

IV	V	VI
History, Philosophy, and Social Foundations	Professional Skills	Educational Institutions

Financing Public Elementary and Secondary Education

HOWARD R. JONES

Dean, College of Education
University of Iowa

The Center for Applied Research in Education, Inc.
New York

© 1966 BY THE CENTER FOR APPLIED
RESEARCH IN EDUCATION, INC.
NEW YORK

ALL RIGHTS RESERVED. NO PART OF THIS BOOK
MAY BE REPRODUCED IN ANY FORM, BY MIMEO-
GRAPH OR ANY OTHER MEANS, WITHOUT PER-
MISSION IN WRITING FROM THE PUBLISHERS.

LIBRARY OF CONGRESS
CATALOG CARD NO.: 66-19210

PRINTED IN THE UNITED STATES OF AMERICA

Foreword

Two approaches have marked the study of educational finance. Traditionally, attention has been focused upon the sources of funds and their disbursement. More recently, study has been given to the economics of educational finance—in an effort to identify education as a major social phenomenon and as a factor of production in the total economy. This book encompasses both these approaches.

Dr. Jones has organized this volume in such a manner that the reader has an opportunity to review pertinent statistics; gain an understanding of both the basic principles involved in educational finance and of the major issues involved in the administration of state school support. The reader is introduced to ways local, state, and federal governments finance education at both the elementary and secondary levels.

The author deals very effectively with this diverse government participation in educational finance and with the problems involved. Each chapter opens with a concise listing of the major topics to be treated therein. Then a brief—but fundamental—discussion follows.

By relating the basic facts of financial support and the issues involved to the structure of the three levels of our government, Dr. Jones has made a major contribution in this field.

School administrators, teachers, members of school boards, members of parent-school groups, and other laymen will learn and benefit by reading *Financing Public Elementary and Secondary Education*.

HOWARD S. BRETSCH

*Professor of Educational Administration
and Associate Dean, Graduate School
The University of Michigan*

Financing Public Elementary and Secondary Education

Howard R. Jones

The problems of how to finance American public schools has long challenged many of our nation's best minds. How to solve these problems is the basic theme of Howard R. Jones' monograph *Financing Public Elementary and Secondary Education.*

Dr. Jones has written a competent book dealing with a difficult field. It is a comprehensive primer on school finance and contains far more information than most books many times its size.

Opening with a description of the American economy and the expenditures involved in public education, the book next incorporates research done by Paul Mort and others indicating how great the need is for financial support of public education. The book goes on exploring the full range of problems, issues, and guidelines for state school support.

Local financial support such as the property tax is analyzed; state taxation methods are examined; and then federal government support is taken into consideration. The final chapter is both comprehensive and analytical as it places in perspective the efforts made by the federal government to finance public education.

Dr. Jones writes with rich educational experience as background having been a teacher, a superintendent of schools, a university professor, a college president, and now is Dean of the College of Education at the University of Iowa. His book deserves the close attention of school administrators, state education department personnel, school board members, students of school administration, and laymen interested in education. *Financing Public Elementary and Secondary Education* well deserves a place in the Library of Education.

DANIEL E. GRIFFITHS

Content Editor

Contents

CHAPTER I

The American Economy and Expenditures for Public Education   1

The Costs of Education and the Revenue Sources   1
Demands for Financing Schools in the Years Ahead   5
The Capacity of the Economy to Support Increasing Public School Expenditures   9
Education as an Investment   11

CHAPTER II

The Measurement of Fiscal Need   15

The Cost-Quality Relation   15
A Foundation Program for School Support   18
Determination of Costs in a Foundation Program   19
Proposal of the Educational Policies Commission for Determining Minimum Cost   20

CHAPTER III

Guidelines for State School Support   28

CHAPTER IV

Issues and Problems in the Administration of State Support   40

Issues Underlying a State Plan for Financing Education   40
Problems in the Administration of State Support Programs   56

CONTENTS

CHAPTER V

Local Revenues in the Financing of Public Schools   58

Sources of Local Revenue for Schools	58
Determination of Property Subject to Taxation	60
Assessment of the Value of Property for Tax Purposes	62
Establishment of a Tax Rate	67
Collection of Property Taxes	70
Non-Property Taxes for Public Schools	71
School District Organization in Relation to Local Revenues	73
The Property Tax: Maligned but Munificent	75

CHAPTER VI

State Taxation for Public Schools   77

Sources of State Revenues	77
Allocation of State Funds to Education	80
Differences Between the States in State Support of Schools and in Taxing Capacity	81
Trends in State School Support	83

CHAPTER VII

The Role of Federal Government in Financing Education   85

Federal Measures for Financial Assistance to Education	85
Summary of the Role of the Federal Government	100
Pros and Cons of Federal Aid to Education	102
Ancillary Issues Concerning Federal Aid	106

Bibliography   111

Index   113

*Financing Public Elementary
and Secondary Education*

CHAPTER I

The American Economy and Expenditures for Public Education

When school opens in the fall of each year, forty million pupils enter public elementary and secondary schools in the United States. These students, representing one-fifth of the total population, are taught by more than a million and a half teachers. The task of school administration claims the services of more than a hundred thousand principals, supervisors, and superintendents.

The various volumes of *The Library of Education* examine many facets of this tremendous enterprise. It is the purpose of this book to explore the means by which public elementary and secondary schools are supported and to discuss major issues which emerge from the practices and patterns of educational finance.

This first chapter seeks to answer these questions:

- What do our public schools cost, and from what governmental agencies are our schools financed?
- What demands for financing schools must be faced in the years ahead?
- What is the capacity of the economy to support increasing public school expenditures?
- What is the relation between education and economic productivity? To what extent can education expenditures be represented as an investment?

The Costs of Education and the Revenue Sources

Table 1 presents the costs of education for selected years from 1949–66. The costs include expenditures for new school buildings. The cost of current operating expenses exclusive of capital outlay would be about four-fifths of the total costs shown.

TABLE 1

TOTAL AND PER PUPIL EXPENDITURES FOR PUBLIC ELEMENTARY AND SECONDARY EDUCATION IN THE UNITED STATES, SELECTED YEARS, 1949-50 to 1965-66[1]

School year	Total expenditures	Expenditures per pupil in average daily attendance
1949–50	$ 5,837,643,000	$259
1951–52	7,344,237,000	313
1953–54	9,092,449,000	351
1955–56	10,955,047,000	388
1957–58	13,569,163,000	449
1959–60	15,613,255,000	472
1961–62[2]	18,373,339,000	530
1963–64[2]	21,444,434,000	573
1965–66[3]	25,824,635,000	659

While the increase in costs may seem very substantial, with total expenditures more than doubling in the last ten years and per pupil costs increasing by nearly 70 per cent, this gain is dwarfed when a comparison is made between expenditures for education now and at the turn of the century. The costs of education in unadjusted dollars expended have increased more than sixty-fold since 1900. Of course, the term "unadjusted dollars" tells a major part of the story, and so do the enrollment figures which, for elementary and secondary school pupils in average daily attendance, have increased more than three-fold.

Werner Hirsch completed a study in 1959 in which he attempted to obtain as just a comparison as possible of educational expenditures from 1900 to 1958. Costs of auxiliary services were dropped from his tabulations because the schools of 1900 had no school buses, were not served by school cafeterias, and had few expenditures for school health services. The study sought "to measure the

---

[1] Office of Education, "Progress of Public Education in the United States of America 1963-64," *Report of the Office of Education, U.S. Department of Health, Education, and Welfare to the Twenty-Seventh International Conference on Public Education, Geneva, Switzerland, July 6-17, 1964*. Washington: U.S. Government Printing Office, 1964, Table 12, p. 18.

[2] Data for expenditures and pupils in average daily attendance for 1961-62 and 1963-64 from *Statistical Summary of State School Systems, 1963-64*. Washington: U.S. Government Printing Office 1965, Table 2, p. 10, Table 8, p. 22. Per pupil expenditures derived from these data.

[3] Data for expenditures and pupils in average daily attendance for 1965-66 are estimates from *Estimates of School Statistics, 1965-66*. Research Report 1965-R17. Washington: National Education Association, 1965, pp. 10, 19.

EXPENDITURES FOR PUBLIC EDUCATION 3

cost of an education unit so standardized that its variety and scope are held reasonably constant, and expressed in per pupil in average daily attendance terms."[4] Salary levels for all of the years were made constant by adjusting them to the "expenditures that would have been incurred if 1954 salary conditions had prevailed throughout the period."[5] Adjustments were also made for the length of the school year, which has increased markedly since 1900. Hirsch thus ended up with a daily per pupil expenditure figure in terms of 1954 dollars. He concluded that

> Costs in real terms exhibit amazing stability during 1900–1958. For the years for which data are available, 1922 was the low year with $1.37 daily expenditure per pupil, and 1913 was the high year with $1.60. Over the 58 years, an overall decline of about 3 per cent was registered.[6]

The distribution of expenditures by account headings which have

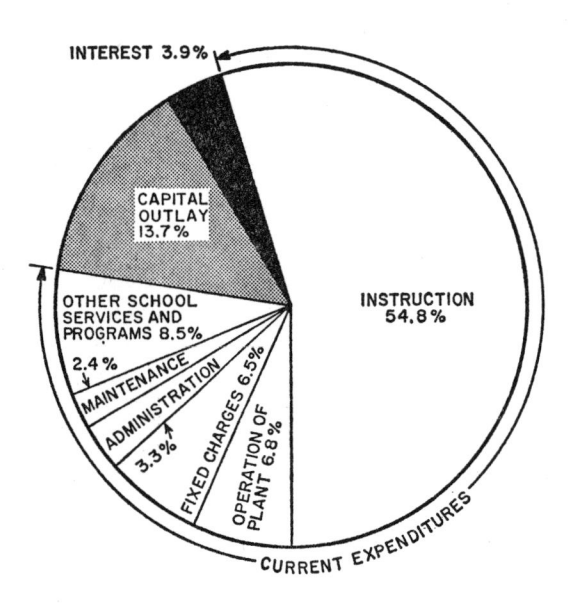

Figure 1. Percentage Distribution of Expenditures for Public Elementary and Secondary Schools, United States, 1963-64. (From data presented in Statistical Summary of State School Systems, 1963-64, Washington: U.S. Government Printing Office, 1965, p. 6.) Percentages do not total exactly 100% due to rounding.

INTEREST 3.9%
CAPITAL OUTLAY 13.7%
OTHER SCHOOL SERVICES AND PROGRAMS 8.5%
2.4%
MAINTENANCE
ADMINISTRATION 3.3%
FIXED CHARGES 6.5%
OPERATION OF PLANT 6.8%
INSTRUCTION 54.8%
CURRENT EXPENDITURES

---

[4] Werner A. Hirsch, "Analysis of Rising Costs of Public Education," *Study Paper No. 4*, Materials Prepared in Connection with the Study of Employment, Growth, and Price Levels for consideration by the Joint Economic Committee, Congress of the United States. Washington: U.S. Government Printing Office, 1959, p. 33.
[5] *Ibid.*
[6] *Ibid.*, p. 34.

become standard for budgeting and accounting is shown for 1963–64 in Figure 1. This graph includes expenditures for capital outlay. The percentage distribution for current expenditures when capital outlay and interest expenses are deducted is shown in Table 2.

TABLE 2

PERCENTAGE DISTRIBUTION OF CURRENT EXPENDITURES FOR PUBLIC ELEMENTARY AND SECONDARY SCHOOLS, 1963–64, BY MAJOR ACCOUNT HEADINGS REFLECTING THE PURPOSE OF THE EXPENDITURES[7]

Purpose	Per cent distribution
Administration	4.1
Instruction	68.2
Plant operation	8.5
Plant maintenance	3.0
Fixed charges	8.1
Other school services (includes expenditures for attendance services, health services, pupil transportation, food services, and extracurricular activities)	8.1

Public schools are almost entirely dependent on tax sources for the the revenues which support them. These tax sources are tapped by three levels of government—local, state, and national. The percentage of revenues coming from each of these sources is shown in Figure 2.

It will be noted that before 1930, local property taxes paid for more than four-fifths of the cost of education. Between 1930 and 1950 state sources supplied an increasing proportion of school revenues. Since 1950, the proportion of revenues derived from state and local sources has remained relatively constant, although the percentage from local revenue sources has declined somewhat. Federal assistance has shown a marked increase, however, particularly as the result of the Elementary and Secondary Education Act of 1965.

Demands for Financing Schools in the Years Ahead

One of the major pressures which demands larger appropriations for schools is the increasing enrollments which continually inundate

---

[7] Data for this table taken from *Statistical Summary of State School Systems, 1963–64, op. cit.,* p. 2.

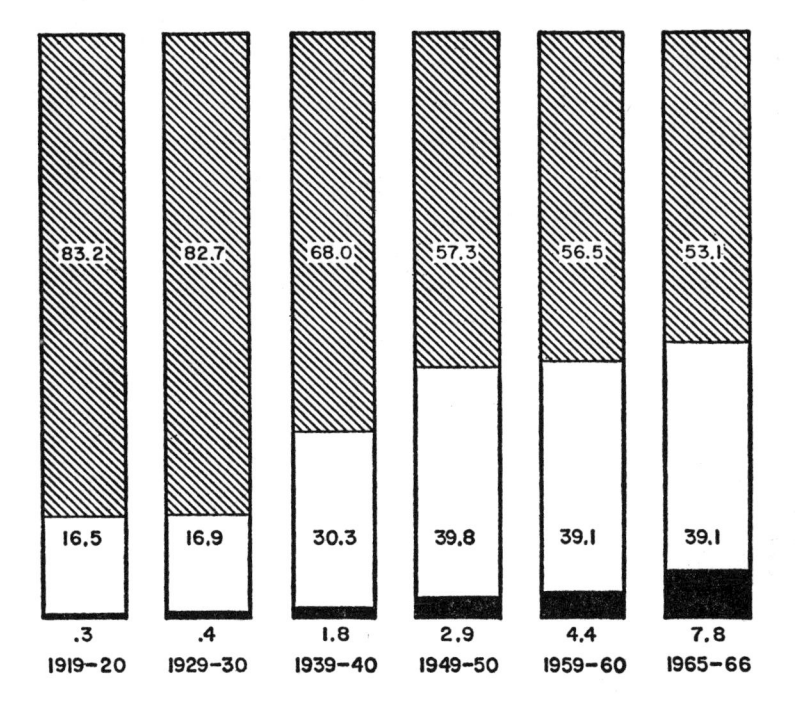

EXPENDITURES FOR PUBLIC EDUCATION 5

	1919-20	1929-30	1939-40	1949-50	1959-60	1965-66
Local	83.2	82.7	68.0	57.3	56.5	53.1
State	16.5	16.9	30.3	39.8	39.1	39.1
Federal	.3	.4	1.8	2.9	4.4	7.8

Figure 2.
Per cent of Public Elementary and Secondary School Revenue Derived from Local, State, and Federal Sources, Selected Years 1919-20 to 1965-66.[8]

CODE: ■ FEDERAL SOURCES □ STATE SOURCES ▨ LOCAL SOURCES

Per cent figures for federal sources appear immediately below their portion of the bar graph.

the schools, taxing the physical plant and requiring more teachers than are being prepared in teacher education institutions. And enrollment growth in the last twelve years foretells more of the same yet to come.

---

[8] Data for all but the 1965–66 school year from Carol Joy Hobson and Samuel Schloss, *Statistics of State School Systems, 1959–60*. U.S. Office of Education Circular No. 691. Washington: U.S. Government Printing Office, 1963, Table G, p. 13. 1965–66 data are estimated and are from *Estimates of School Statistics, 1965–66*, Research Report 1965-R17, National Education Association, *op. cit.*, p. 32.

Because of rounding, the per cent distribution may not add exactly to 100%.

TABLE 3
SUMMARY OF FALL ENROLLMENTS IN PUBLIC ELEMENTARY AND SECONDARY SCHOOLS, FIFTY STATES AND THE DISTRICT OF COLUMBIA, 1954–65[9]

Year	Total	Elementary	Secondary
1954	29,548,805	21,310,096	8,238,709
1955	30,680,183	22,159,143	8,521,040
1956	31,718,732	22,216,495	9,502,237
1957	32,951,426	22,860,801	10,090,625
1958	34,080,844	23,414,947	10,665,897
1959	35,182,343	23,906,367	11,275,976
1960	36,281,294	24,349,932	11,931,362
1961	37,464,074	24,603,352	12,860,722
1962	38,748,907	25,263,661	13,485,246
1963	40,217,215	25,816,893	14,400,322
1964	41,416,289	26,221,705	15,194,584
1965	41,700,000	26,379,000	15,321,000

Forecasts for the future are risky. In 1962 a U.S. Office of Education publication attempted a projection of school enrollments through 1980 based on four series of assumptions about demographic factors and extending enrollments from the population data for the decade 1950–1960. Projections were cast in four different ranges, the range of greatest increase being labeled Series A (higher than trend projections). The assumptions were:

> Fertility rates will be higher than the 1955–57 level, enrollment rates will be somewhat higher than trend, and the percentage of enrollment in nonpublic schools will follow trend.[10]

The estimates derived for fall enrollments (Series A) in public elementary and secondary schools are as follows:[11]

1964	41,340,000 total enrollment
1969	46,039,000 total enrollment
1974	51,698,000 total enrollment
1979	58,397,000 total enrollment

---

[9] Data for 1954–61 from Carol Joy Hobson and Samuel Schloss, *Enrollment, Teachers, and Schoolhousing.* U.S. Office of Education Circular No. 703. Washington: Government Printing Office, 1963, p. 32.

Data for 1962 and 1963 from Carol Joy Hobson and Samuel Schloss, *Enrollment, Teachers, and Schoolhousing.* U.S. Office of Education Circular No. 735. Washington: Government Printing Office, 1964, p. 19.

Data for 1964 and 1965 from Kenneth A. Simon and W. Vance Grant, *Digest of Educational Statistics, 1965 Edition.* U.S. Office of Education Bulletin 1965, No. 4. Washington: Government Printing Office, 1965, p. 5. Figures for 1965 are estimates.

[10] Kenneth A. Simon, *Enrollment in Public and Nonpublic Elementary and Secondary Schools, 1950–80,* U.S. Office of Education Circular No. 692. Washington: Government Printing Office, 1962, p. 1.

[11] *Ibid.,* Table 2, p. 7.

Several years have elapsed since 1960, the last year of the decade which could serve as the springboard for the projections. Actual figures for 1964, which are now available, show an enrollment of 41,416,289 pupils (cf. Table 3). This figure exceeds the highest estimate made in the projections for fall enrollment for 1964.

One of the major factors in the continuing growth of elementary school enrollments, and ultimately of secondary school enrollments, is that the young people born at the beginning of the postwar baby boom in 1946 are becoming of marriageable age and the whole cycle is about to begin again. The birth rate per thousand population is actually declining, but the large number of young people who will be establishing families in the years immediately ahead will tend to offset the birth-rate decline. Since the relatively small number of young people who were born in the depression years of the 1930s were responsible for the flooding of schools in the postwar period, what will happen now that their many children are having children of their own? Table 4 shows trends since 1920. Contrast the births before 1945 with the births after 1945.

TABLE 4

NUMBER OF BIRTHS AND BIRTH RATE PER THOUSAND POPULATION, SELECTED YEARS, 1920–1964[12]

Year	No. of Births	Birth rate per thousand population
1920	1,509,000	23.7
1925	1,879,000	21.3
1930	2,204,000	18.9
1935	2,155,000	16.9
1940	2,360,000	17.9
1945	2,735,000	19.5
1950	3,554,000	23.6
1955	4,047,000	24.6
1957	4,255,000	25.0
1958	4,204,000	24.3
1959	4,245,000	24.0
1960	4,258,000	23.7
1961	4,268,000	23.3
1962	4,167,000	22.4
1963	4,098,000	21.7
1964	4,054,000	21.2

[12] U.S. Department of Commerce, Bureau of the Census, *Statistical Abstract of the United States, 1963.* Washington: U.S. Government Printing Office, 1963, p. 52 (for data 1920–1962). *Ibid.,* 1965 Edition, p. 48 (for data for 1963 and 1964).

The number of births in each year is rounded off to the nearest thousand. Data for 1957–63 are based on a 50 per cent sample. 1964 figures are provisional.

In all probability, public elementary and secondary school enrollments will increase by about a third in the next ten years. If, in addition, per pupil costs increase dollarwise as much as they have in the last ten years, these two factors will require expenditures for public elementary and secondary education about double what they are at present.

Furthermore, there are other major factors which are likely to contribute to the increase in the cost of education. The backlog of additional classrooms needed dates back before the war years. While this backlog is being slowly reduced, more than 120,000 additional classrooms are still needed if pupils are to be adequately housed in classes which are not excessive in size.[13]

The teacher shortage has become chronic. Each year more than 80,000 teachers with less than standard certificates are employed because fully qualified teachers are not available.[14] The critical factor in this shortage is the competition among professions and occupations to secure superior young men and young women graduating from our colleges each year. While salary levels have increased substantially in the last decade, salary is still an important factor in recruitment, and there is no question but that salaries must continue to rise in the years ahead. To retain career teachers, it is particularly important that maximum salary levels be raised. In most professions, maximum salaries are at least double the minimum salaries, whereas for public school teachers maximum salaries are approximately 50 per cent higher than minimum salaries for teachers with bachelor's degrees, approximately 65 per cent higher for teachers who earn master's degrees.

The postwar birth-rate increase has already hit the high schools and, indeed, the colleges with the full weight of its impact. Since the population wave first reached the high schools, secondary school enrollments have been increasing at a greater rate than elementary school enrollments. This, coupled with the greater retention of pupils through the high school years, has meant that the largest percentage enrollment increases are taking place at the school level at which costs are highest. For the next decade this fact will continue to contribute to the mounting cost of education.

---

[13] Carol Joy Hobson and Samuel Schloss, Circular No. 735, 1964, *op. cit.*, Table 14, p. 32.
[14] *Ibid.*, Table 3, p. 12.

All of this would be overwhelming, except that a backward glance shows resilience and responsiveness to educational needs. If predictions had been made in public a decade ago that expenditures for elementary and secondary schools would double in the next ten years, the speaker would likely have been termed either an alarmist or a dreamer. Yet dollar expenditures for education in 1963–64 were more than two and a quarter times the expenditures for education in 1953–54.[15] What is so frequently overlooked is that the economy of the country is growing also, and that future growth need not be predicated upon present revenue levels.

The Capacity of the Economy to Support Increasing Public School Expenditures

A measure frequently used as a yardstick of economic growth is the gross national product, which is defined as the value of goods and services produced. Table 5 shows the growth in the gross na-

TABLE 5

The Increase in the Gross National Product, Selected Years 1950–1964, and the Educational Expenditures for Public Elementary and Secondary Schools as Per Cent of the Gross National Product[16]

Calendar year	Gross national product	School year	Expenditures for education	Educational expenditures as per cent of gross national product
1950	$284,599,000,000	1949–50	$ 5,837,643,000	2.1
1952	346,999,000,000	1951–52	7,344,237,000	2.1
1954	363,112,000,000	1953–54	9,092,449,000	2.5
1956	419,180,000,000	1955–56	10,955,047,000	2.6
1958	444,546,000,000	1957–58	13,569,163,000	3.1
1960	502,601,000,000	1959–60	15,613,255,000	3.1
1962	556,199,000,000	1961–62	18,169,057,000	3.3
1964	633,500,000,000 (Est.)	1963–64	21,444,434,000	3.4

[15] *Supra,* Table 1, p. 2.
[16] Figures for the gross national product (in millions of dollars) taken from U.S. Department of Commerce, Office of Business Economics, "National Income and Product, 1963," *Survey of Current Business,* XLIV (July 1964), 8. Estimate for 1964 from *Survey of Current Business,* XLV (January 1965), 15.
Educational expenditures are those in Table 1, *supra,* p. 2.
The two different sets of data, gross national product and educational expenditures, are based on slightly different calendar periods—the calendar year and the school year. Data for exactly comparable periods are not available.

tional product since 1950 and relates this growth to educational expenditures.

It is seen that the costs of education since 1950 have increased at a more rapid rate than the growth in the economy as measured by the gross national product. The Committee on Educational Finance of the National Education Association has cast data of this nature in terms of current prices and has computed annual growth rates. It reports that the average annual growth rate of school expenditures during the last ten years has been 1.7 times the average annual rate of increase in the gross national product.[17] These figures attest a growing effort to support education—but it is not an extraordinary effort. There were many years in the depth of the depression when educational costs were more than 3.5 per cent of the gross national product.

Looking at the years immediately ahead, one can estimate that the needs of public elementary and secondary education can be met if between 4 and 5 per cent of the annual increase in the gross national product can be channeled into education—assuming the present rate of growth in the economy. If this rate should be speeded up, which is not unlikely, a lower per cent would suffice. Of course, one should recognize that approximately four-fifths of the increase in the national production should probably remain in the private sector of the economy. The needs of education, then, may call for as much as one-fourth or one-fifth of the increase in the national production which is utilized in the public sector of the economy. Whether this will be feasible depends on the international situation and the needs of defense, the space program, foreign aid, roads, and all other governmental services.

In the final analysis the question is one of values. As a nation the United States spends more for recreation, more for transportation, and more for tobacco and alcoholic beverages than it does for education. In testifying before a congressional committee in 1959, Walter Heller stated succinctly:

> The underlying capacity exists, provided the American people have the will to allot somewhat more of their growing income to educat-

---

[17] Committee on Educational Finance, National Education Association, *Financial Status of the Public Schools, 1964*. Washington, D.C.: National Education Association, 1964, p. 15.

ing their children and somewhat less to frivolities, indulgences, and luxuries.[18]

Education as an Investment

Thus far in this monograph the costs of education have been represented largely as expenses incurred but with little reference as to the goals these expenditures serve or to the dividends which these expenditures yield.

The non-monetary outcomes of education are, of course, the most important: the opportunity for each individual to find and establish a value framework, to realize his intellectual capabilities, to prepare for a life work utilizing his capacities, to establish the interpersonal relationships that enable him to be an effective member of the community in which he lives. For society, these non-monetary outcomes include the educated citizenry upon which democracy depends, the collective intelligence to cope with each generation's problems, the dedication to values which give primacy to the worth of each human being.

Over and above these results of education—which by themselves are justification for the investment—are related outcomes which have an economic significance in increased economic productivity, justifying the assertion that the money invested in education results in a yield *in monetary dividends* which more than repays the principal invested.

Efforts are sometimes made to illustrate this economic return by comparing the college graduate, in terms of lifetime earnings, with those who completed their formal schooling at the end of the twelfth grade and with those who terminated schooling with the eighth grade. Probably the best study of this character, made by Herman P. Miller, presents data showing that on the average the high school graduate will earn in his lifetime some $76,000 more than the student who terminates his schooling with completion of the eighth grade. Similarly, the lifetime earnings of the college graduate will average some $177,000 more than the lifetime earnings of the student whose schooling ends with graduation from high school. Miller

---

[18] Walter W. Heller, "It's Up to Congress: Education is a National Responsibility." Testimony before the Subcommittee on Education of the Senate Committee on Labor and Public Welfare, February 5, 1959. Published by the NEA Legislative Commission. Washington: National Education Association, 1959, p. 6.

shows that the relative income differentials for those with different levels of schooling have been maintained down through the years and that they have not lessened even with higher percentages of students completing high school and college.[19]

Studies such as this, however, are limited by the fact that all of the variables that operate to influence the relationship between schooling and income cannot be controlled. While there undoubtedly is a causal relationship between amount of education and lifetime earnings, there are other contributing factors. Those with higher intelligence tend to continue their education, and their success in remunerative employment is due in part to native ability as well as to breadth and depth of education. Even when intelligence is factored out, there are motivational and emotional factors that condition both continuation in schooling and earnings in employment. It is true, too, that a college degree has become a *sine qua non* for entry into some of the positions commanding higher salaries, so that a free market does not exist where ability and potentiality can be displayed regardless of formal education. Even with these cautions, however, the relationship between education and earnings is so striking that it seems reasonable to impute a substantial dollar return to the investment made in education. This is true even when the amount of money invested in education includes not only the cost paid by government funds but also the earnings foregone by the individual while continuing education into the years of possible employment.

Another approach to the study of education as an investment is the measurement of its impact on the economic structure as a whole, rather than of returns to the individual. It has been very evident in recent years that economic growth cannot be attributed entirely to land, labor, and physical capital—the major factors of production stipulated by Adam Smith when he drew together the first comprehensive picture of the market economy. Economists have found a greater "output" in economic growth than could have been predicted from the measured "inputs" of land, labor, and capital, as these factors have been traditionally measured. A substantial part of the unexplained growth seems due to the improved quality of human resources. "Human capital," a new term, has been coined to reflect

---

[19] Herman P. Miller, "Annual and Lifetime Income in Relation to Education," *American Economic Review*, L (December 1960), 962–86.

the component of advancing technology and new discoveries resulting from research and to include the improved skills and knowledge possessed by management and the labor force. Efforts have been made to quantify this investment in human capital and to refine measures of its yield in terms of increased economic return. Some of the conclusions of those immersed in these studies are:

> ... private research to date suggests that the average rate of return on investment in formal education as a whole is higher than the rate of return for business investment.[20]
>
> In economic terms, the marginal efficiency of investment in human capital is currently higher in our society than the marginal efficiency of investment in physical capital.[21]
>
> ... whereas physical capital contributed almost twice that of education between 1909 and 1929, the contribution of education to economic growth between 1929 and 1957 exceeded that of physical capital.[22]
>
> ... a dollar or a rupee invested in the intellectual improvement of human beings will regularly bring a greater increase in national income than a dollar or a rupee devoted to railways, dams, machine tools, or other tangible capital goods.[23]
>
> Especially since World War II, economists are discovering that growth may be mainly a matter of developing human talent and that it can be deliberately fostered by judicious but generous allocation of resources for this purpose.[24]

There is other evidence of the relationship between education and economic development. John K. Norton has presented a number of studies showing the relationship between education and economic development in the various countries of the world. His data show a

---

[20] Walter W. Heller, "Education as an Instrument of Economic Policy." Address delivered before the O.E.C.D. Policy Conference on Economic Growth and Investment in Education, Washington, D.C., October 18, 1961, p. 4 of mimeographed text of address.

[21] Eugene L. Swearingen, "Education as an Investment," *Financing the Changing School Program*. Washington: Committee on Educational Finance, National Education Association, 1962, p. 20.

[22] Theodore W. Schultz, "Reflections on Investment in Man," *The Journal of Political Economy* (Chicago: University of Chicago Press) Supplement LXX (October, 1962), 5. © 1962 by the University of Chicago. Schultz is commenting on both his own studies and studies by Edward F. Denison.

[23] John K. Galbraith, quoted in Arthur Schlesinger, Jr., "The One Against the Many," *Saturday Review*, XLV (July 14, 1962), 9.

[24] Harold M. Groves, *Education and Economic Growth*. Washington: The Committee on Educational Finance, National Education Association, 1961, p. 7.

strong positive correlation between measures of educational development (such as extent of literacy and educational expenditures per capita) and measures of economic development (such as per capita income). Norton's basic conclusion was formulated more than twenty years ago, with more recent studies attesting its validity:

> ... the experiences of the nations of the world and the findings of technical statistical investigations unite in supporting the hypothesis that high productivity and adequate education go together and that the latter does have important effects on the former.[25]

---

[25] John K. Norton, *Education and Economic Well-Being in American Democracy*. Washington: Educational Policies Commission, National Education Association, 1940, p. 30.

CHAPTER II

The Measurement of Fiscal Need

- Does more money for schools result in better education?
- What is a foundation program for school support?
- How may a foundation program be determined?

The Cost-Quality Relation

What education does our money buy? If we spend more for our educational programs, will our children receive better education? These are basic questions and ones to which researchers in school finance have long sought answers. A major stumbling block which still stands in the way of definitive and unconditional answers is the fact that the direct outcomes of education are very difficult to measure. If this were not so, programs of merit rating would long since have been established in schools. Education as reflected in knowledge of subject matter has been measured with fair exactitude and the ability to apply that subject matter, particularly in life situations, has been partially measured. But the ability to think creatively as a result of the instructional program has not yet been measured with validity. The measurement of attitudes, loyalties, and values, and the extent to which they are an outgrowth of the instructional program has barely been tapped. Many of the outcomes of education are not fully demonstrated until a young person enters the responsibilities of adulthood; many of them are the fruits of home, church, peer groups, mass media, and many other influences, all intertwined with the direct results of the school program. For these reasons, studies of cost-quality relations in education have had to rely on secondary measures of quality. These secondary measures are similar to the criteria which have been developed by accrediting associations for judging school systems. For example, do those schools which spend more money on education have better teachers? (Better teachers may be defined as those who hold at least a bachelor's degree and who have had a program of preparation encompassing a broad general education, advanced preparation in the subject fields to be taught, and professional work leading to knowledge of the child, the learning process, and the instructional program.) Researchers have taken what has been measurable in terms of presumed quality and have related it to educational costs.

Among the factors which have been used as indicative of quality in education are effective teaching of tool subjects, diversification of curriculum permitting opportunities for exploration of abilities, relatively high amount of individual attention received by children, provision of programs of guidance and counseling, progression from grade to grade with little retardation, holding power through completion of high school, longer school terms, relatively high percentage of children entering college, excellence of physical plant, and provision of supplies and materials for instruction. These characteristics are rarely used singly; rather, a combination of these and other factors is usually found in any instrument purporting to measure educational quality because some of the indices presuming to measure quality of education may, when used by themselves, be more strongly indicative of other factors. For example, percentage of young people entering college may reflect the intelligence levels of the children or the socio-economic status of their parents as well as excellence of schooling.

One of the most interesting tools used in measuring quality of education assumes that the extent to which schools incorporate newer methods of teaching and of administration reflects quality. The instrument entitled *The Growing Edge* is characterized as an index of the adaptability of school systems. The responsiveness of schools to newer approaches is measured in four dimensions:

1. The teaching of skills in a real or realistic fashion and the teaching of a wider range of skills;
2. The teaching of areas of knowledge realistically;
3. The discovery and development of special aptitudes of individuals through test and try-out;
4. The development of gross behavior patterns, such as citizenship, character, and thinking, which are assumed to be developmental characteristics.[1]

When these factors were quantified and combined in an over-all

---

[1] Paul R. Mort, Walter C. Reusser, and John W. Polley, *Public School Finance, Its Background, Structure and Operation*. New York: McGraw-Hill Book Company, Inc., Third Edition, 1960, pp. 81–82.

THE MEASUREMENT OF FISCAL NEED

score, a correlation of .59 was found to exist with the expenditure level of schools.[2]

An elaborate study of the American high school involving more than 1300 schools, although not designed primarily as a research project in the cost-quality relationship, did seek to establish factors associated with a good high school. It defined a good high school in terms of pupil achievement, holding power, and percentage of able young people entering college. Four basic factors found to be associated with the "good school" were teachers' salaries, years of experience of the teaching staff, number of volumes in the school library, and expenditures per pupil.[3] It will be noted that all four of these items are cost items. Higher teachers' salaries, greater experience of staff, and a larger number of books in the library are components of over-all pupil expenditure.

From the studies attempting to relate cost and quality, certain conclusions may be drawn:

1. The relationship between cost and quality is most evident at the extremes. Schools of highest quality almost invariably rank high in cost per pupil. Schools of low cost are rarely above the lowest quartile in quality. In the middle of the distribution there are many factors, including the quality of the educational leadership, that appear to operate to vary the placement of schools on a quality index in relation to expenditures.
2. Some schools of high cost are not schools of quality. There still are a large number of school districts with inadequate secondary school programs due to limited enrollment. Some of these are high cost districts which rank low on quality indices.
3. When increasing funds have been provided school districts of high quality which are in the upper end of the cost distribution *over a period of years,* the increasing funds continue to result in increasing educational return. It would seem that there must be a point of diminishing returns, but this point is not yet in sight.
4. Considering the spectrum as a whole, increasing expenditures for schools do not automatically, immediately, and in direct proportion bring about an increased quality of education. Increasing returns tend to lag behind investments. Adaptability studies show that schools change slowly. Furno reports that "the effect of an expenditure-level quality change is measurable even after twenty-

---

[2] *Ibid.,* p. 82.
[3] Reported in *Education U.S.A.,* weekly publication of the National School Public Relations Association, March 21, 1963, p. 1.

five years, and that the maximum impact occurs in about seven years."[4]

5. Although the instruments developed to measure quality are far from perfect, and although no single factor by itself correlates highly with measures of quality, the one factor which consistently appears at the top of the positive correlations in study after study is educational expenditure, usually expressed in cost per pupil.

6. The generalization seems warranted that high quality schools do require above average expenditures. Although above average expenditures alone do not guarantee good schools, low investments in education do tend to doom schools to mediocre programs.

A Foundation Program for School Support

In spite of the imperfect relationship demonstrated between cost and quality by the studies just summarized, it is evident that "bricks cannot be made without straw" and that funds must be provided if schools are to fulfill their task. There must be a minimum level—sometimes characterized as the foundation program of school support—which every school system should have.

Initially the foundation program referred to the proportion of funds which the state paid the local school system, expecting that on this foundation the rest of the structure of school support would be erected by the local school district. Whatever funds were received by school districts from the state were termed the foundation amount. In recent years, the term "foundation" has taken on the concept of the basic fundamental financial support which should be provided for the education of each child without regard to the particular source of support, whether state or local. In other words, discussion now centers on a foundation program of education representing a floor level of educational opportunity which should be available to every child and on the dollars and cents needed to fund that floor level. School districts may tax themselves to go beyond this floor level in order to provide an educational program richer than that envisaged in the foundation program, but no child should be denied the essentials defined in the foundation level of educational opportunity.

---

[4] Reported in Paul R. Mort, Walter C. Reusser, and John W. Polley, *op. cit.*, p. 86.

Determination of Costs in a Foundation Program

The amount of money necessary to finance the program which should be provided all students has generally been determined in one of two ways. In the first plan, educational costs in typical districts of average wealth in any given state are taken as a yardstick. The effort is made to boost all school programs to at least the level provided by the average districts. The assumption is that the educational services provided by these typical districts are those which the citizens in these communities have weighed and have found necessary. With their average wealth, they consider this level of education worthy of their support. The support figure is usually expressed in terms of cost per pupil. This method of establishing a cost figure for a foundation program represents a relatively easy computation, but it is subject to at least one criticism. After a plan of support such as this is established, what happens to the average? If provisions are made to upgrade the plan periodically to new averages, there is a built-in escalator of costs which cannot easily be justified.

A second procedure used in determining costs is to define the educational services and facilities which should be provided and then to attach a dollar value to these services and facilities. The nature and extent of the services and facilities which should be provided are a matter of subjective judgment, and key lay citizens, including legislators along with professional personnel, are often involved in making the value decisions which present themselves. Some of the basic decisions to be made include judgments as to the qualifications of teachers desired and the probable cost figures necessary to secure teachers with these qualifications, the pupil-teacher ratio to be incorporated in the formula, and the basis on which counseling services and library services will be made available.

Corbally presents a somewhat simplified illustration showing how dollar figures may be attached to the facilities and services deemed to be a part of the foundation program:[5]

1. Classroom unit = 30 pupils
2. Classroom requires personal services as follows:

---

[5] John E. Corbally, Jr., *School Finance*. Boston: Allyn and Bacon, Inc., 1962, p. 133.

1 teacher @ $6,000	$6,000
.05 supervisor @ $6,000	300
.10 administrator @ $8,000	800
.05 librarian @ $6,000	300
.05 counselor @ $6,000	300
Total Personal Service	$7,700
3. Supplies, maintenance, operation, and fixed costs equal one-fourth of personal service:	$1,925
4. Transportation, calculated on a pupil-mile basis for students needing transportation:	$ 325
5. A classroom costs $25,000 to build and will last fifty years. Annual depreciation allowance is one-fiftieth of $25,000:	$ 500
6. Total cost of foundation program per classroom unit (1–5):	$10,450

With either the average cost of the typical district or with the services and facilities approach, some adjustments may be necessary because of varying costs between different regions of the state or because schools in which population is very sparse will need a smaller per pupil ratio. Students in programs of special education will be in smaller classes. The costs of secondary education are greater than the costs of elementary education, and differentiation is warranted. These adjustments are usually accomplished by a weighted pupil figure; for example, physically handicapped pupils may be counted as two pupils in the formula, or if a classroom unit figure is used, the number of pupils in the classroom unit may be cut in half. Separate costs may be computed for elementary and secondary education.

The two units commonly used in foundation formulas are either a per pupil or a classroom unit. It will be noted that the example cited from Corbally uses the classroom as the unit of need.

Proposal of the Educational Policies Commission for Determining Minimum Cost

The Educational Policies Commission of the National Education Association believes that there is a minimum floor level of educational expenditure below which an adequate education cannot be purchased. A formula to determine this floor has been proposed. The formula is designed for application at the local school level, but an adaptation of the formula could easily be made to determine a state foundation amount. The formula as advanced by the Educational Policies Commission is outlined below,[6] followed by a suggested adaptation for possible use on a state-wide basis.

Assumptions underlying the formula. The formula is based on these assumptions:

1. A standard can be set for minimum staff size in relation to enrollment.
2. A standard can be set for the starting salary required in any community to attract competent beginning teachers.
3. The average salary of a professional staff can be derived from the level of beginning salaries.
4. Average per pupil expenditure for professional services can be derived from the staff size and the average salary.
5. The per pupil cost of the professional staff can be related to the over-all budget required for current operations.[7]

The use of these assumptions is explained below. Their sequential application in dollar amounts can determine the minimum current expenditure for education which should be provided by any given community.

1. *A standard can be set for minimum staff size in relation to enrollment.*

Since class size may vary widely under differing conditions, the Educational Policies Commission suggests that staff size may be more important than the size of any particular class. The Commission proposes that a minimum standard which may be followed is that there should be fifty professional staff members for every thousand pupils, including counselors, librarians, specialists in remedial work, the school nurse, curriculum consultants, and supervisors among the professional staff members.

On this basis classes would probably average more than twenty-five pupils per class. A high school of 600, for example, would have at least a principal, two counselors, a school librarian, a school nurse, and the part-time services of many other professionals including an assistant principal, a visiting teacher, the school psychologist, the school physician, curriculum consultants, and possibly some

---
[6] Educational Policies Commission of the National Education, *An Essay on Quality in Public Education.* Washington: National Education Association, 1959, pp. 25, 27–29.
[7] *Ibid.*, p. 27.

special teachers such as those working with physically or mentally handicapped pupils. The services of specialists other than classroom teachers would be equal to the full-time services of at least eight people. Including teachers, the high school of 600 could have the full-time equivalent of thirty professional workers—the ratio of one staff member for every twenty pupils proposed by the Commission. Of the thirty professional workers, however, only 22 would be full-time classroom teachers, and the pupil-classroom teacher ratio would be approximately 27:1, which can be defended as a minimum ratio. But teachers in the secondary school usually have at least one period assigned as a preparation period when they are not in direct pupil contact. Furthermore, all classes do not come exactly packaged in economical enrollments. These two factors would cause average class size to be in excess of twenty-seven pupils per class. The Commission points out that in several school systems with superior programs, the staff size ranges up to seventy professionals per thousand pupils.[8]

In the formula, then, the staff ratio used is fifty professionals per one thousand pupils, or one professional for every twenty pupils.

2. *A standard can be set for the starting salary required in any community to attract competent beginning teachers.*

The Commission advocates that each community determine the starting salary needed to attract competent beginning teachers. No dollar amount is suggested. For purposes of illustrating the operation of the formula, typical 1965 data are used, however. A beginning salary of $5,000 is taken as about the average salary paid college graduates entering teaching in the United States in 1965. A further point of reference is that college graduates entering federal employment at a GS–5 level in 1965 received $5,181.[9] For purposes of this example, $5,000 seems a defensible minimum figure. It does not represent the goal of a minimum salary of $6,000 recommended by the National Education Association, and it is pegged at the average college graduate rather than the very able student who should be encouraged to enter teaching.

---

[8] The recommendations of the Educational Policies Commission in relation to size and composition of the school staff are found in *An Essay On Quality in Public Education, ibid.*, pp. 14–17.

[9] GS–5 level specified in Public Law 89–301, Section 2(b), October 29, 1965.

3. *The average salary of a professional staff can be derived from the level of beginning salaries.*

The application of this assumption causes some further postulates to be stated. One supposition is that salary increments will be awarded successful teachers who remain in service, so that the starting salary will double within ten years. Another supposition is that teaching must attract career people—that high turnover in any community thwarts the progressive advancement of the work of the school system. Assuming reasonable balance in a school staff between younger and older teachers, a distribution of the percentage of teachers at different salary levels might be as follows:

 10% of the staff at the starting salary level
 20% at 1.25 times the starting level
 20% at 1.50 times the starting level
 20% at 2.00 times the starting level
 20% at 2.25 times the starting level
 10% at 2.50 times the starting level

In such a distribution, the average salary would be approximately 1.7 times a reasonable, competitive beginning salary for teachers.

4. *Average per pupil expenditure for professional services can be derived from the staff size and the average salary.*

If there should be one professional educator for every twenty pupils, and if the salary of the professional educators in any given community should average 1.7 times the starting salary, the per pupil allotment for professional salaries would be 1.7/20 of the starting salary. Expressed as a percentage, this means that the dollar amount expended per pupil for professional salaries should be in the neighborhood of 8½ per cent of the reasonable beginning salary for a teacher in any given community.

5. *The per pupil cost of the professional staff can be related to the over-all budget required for current operation.*

In the country as a whole, the portion of a school system's budget that is devoted to professional salaries approximates 70 per cent of the total operating (current expense) budget—a figure sometimes advocated as a minimum percentage to be devoted to teachers' salaries. If the minimum per pupil amount which should be spent for professional salaries represents 8½ per cent of the beginning salary of a teacher and if professional salaries represent 70 per cent of total current expenditures, then the minimum per pupil amount which should be set aside for *all* current expenditures should be 12 1/7 per cent of the beginning salary of a teacher (8.5 per cent divided by 70/100). This computation, then, culminates in a simple yardstick which sets forth approximately 12 per cent of the reasonable salary of a beginning teacher as the per pupil amount which should be expended in any given community for the current expenditures of a school system. If a beginning salary of $5,000 is used in applying this formula, the per pupil expenditure for current operations should be at least $600.

Restatement of the formula. The conclusion of the Educational Policies Commission is that:

> In a school district of adequate size the minimum annual per-pupil current expenditure needed today to provide a good educational program is about twelve per cent of the salary necessary to employ a qualified beginning teacher in that district.[10]

The assumptions underlying this formula are open to examination and questioning, of course, but if one accepts them as reasonable, the formula must be accepted as a defensible measure of needed financing.

A modification of this formula for statewide purposes in a foundation program. It would seem that the procedures suggested by the Educational Policies Commission could be adapted to determine a foundation amount for a state aid formula. Simplifying the formula somewhat, the following principles could result in a realistic and defensible basis for determining the amount of money which local school districts and the state should combine to provide for each public school pupil:

1. The salary to be paid teachers is the most critical factor in the determination of any foundation amount. The median salary paid teachers in the state can be used as a starting point in a foundation formula.
2. A per pupil amount for professional instructional services can be determined by adopting a ratio of a stipulated number of pupils per professional staff member.
3. A per pupil amount for all current expenditures can be derived from the cost per pupil for instructional services, using the ratio existing between teachers' salaries and total current expenditures.

---

[10] Educational Policies Commission, *An Essay on Quality in Public Education, op. cit.,* p. 25.

Each of these principles is examined below, with a hypothetical application to illustrate how a foundation amount might be determined.

1. *The salary to be paid teachers is the most critical factor in the determination of any foundation amount. The median salary paid teachers in the state can be used as a starting point in a foundation formula.*

It is proposed that the median salary of teachers in the state for the preceding year, rather than a salary amount for teachers 1.7 times their starting salary, be used as the professional salary figure in the foundation formula. The reasons for this are threefold: the salaries of teachers on a statewide basis for the previous year can be computed accurately and objectively now that machine accounting methods are available to most state departments; the fact that approximately half of the school teachers in the state would have already been paid at this salary level makes the salary figure one which may be recognized as attainable; this figure is more easily understood than the years-of-experience distribution table which undergirds the Policies Commission ratio of 1.7 times the salary of beginning teachers.

This formula might be further refined by determining median teachers' salaries by intermediate school district units, using the median teacher's salary in each intermediate unit for the previous year. The advantage of this is that a factor related somewhat to the cost of education could be built into the formula, for living costs and educational costs may vary in different parts of the state.

For sake of illustration, let us assume that the median salary for teachers in the state for the preceding year is $6,500.

2. *A per pupil amount for professional instructional services can be determined by adopting a ratio of a stipulated number of pupils per professional staff member.*

The ratio advocated by the Educational Policies Commission can be used. The one danger is that the public may construe the twenty to one figure as a figure of class size. It will take careful explaining to demonstrate that for every four or five classroom teachers, there is the equivalent of at least one more professional in the instructional salary category whose presence is necessary to the effective running of a school system.

Let us accept the 20:1 ratio of the Educational Policies Commission for the sake of illustration. With the teacher's salary determined to be $6,500, the per pupil cost for professional instructional services is $325 ($6,500 ÷ 20).

3. *A per pupil amount for all current expenditures can be derived from the cost per pupil for instructional services, using the ratio existing between teachers' salaries and total current expenditures.*

The ratio between teachers' salaries and the total amount spent for current expenditures would not be an estimate. Just as actual salary figures for the previous year were used above, the percentage of total expenditures for the previous year in the state which went for teachers' salaries would be used here. It is likely that this percentage will be closer to 65 per cent than to the 70 per cent used in the Commission formula. Year by year computation would keep this figure accurate; it would be rounded out to the nearest whole per cent.

In the example we are using, let us assume a 65 per cent figure as the percentage of the total operating budget allotted for instructional salaries. The $325 previously determined, then, as the cost of professional instructional service would represent 65 per cent of the total operating budget on a per pupil basis. The foundation amount for current operating expense (100 per cent) can easily be computed ($325 ÷ $\frac{65}{100}$ = $500).

Advantages of this procedure in reaching a foundation amount.

1. It is simple; it is easily computed; it can be understood by the lay public as well as by professional educators.
2. The figures are objectively determined.
3. The same procedure can be used each year. As rising costs increase the cost of education, the formula likewise increases the foundation amount. New legislation to determine a foundation figure would not be needed each year.

Limitations.

1. Capital outlay and bonded indebtedness are not considered in the formula. A separate physical plant program apart from the foundation program for operating expenditures would have to be framed.
2. Teachers' salaries are computed on the basis of what teachers actually are paid, rather than on some basis of what they *ought* to

be paid. A variation from using the median teacher's salary for the previous year would be to take the average salary of all gainfully employed persons in the state for the previous year, multiplying it by an index figure (say 1.5) in view of the greater preparation needed for teaching and the importance of the teaching post. This procedure would preclude the escalator effect which might operate to establish constantly higher median salaries, although it was to minimize this effect that the use of median rather than average salaries was proposed.

Thus far the procedure advanced by the Educational Policies Commission has not received widespread use, even by local school systems. Experimentation with formulas of this character, however, may bring about a new means of deriving amounts to be placed in foundation formulas.

No means of determining the relative share of state and local governments in financing the foundation program once it has been determined have been presented in this chapter. This topic will be dealt with in the next chapter.

CHAPTER III

Guidelines for State School Support

What are the guidelines for state school support in terms of:
- Expressing a foundation program in dollar terms?
- State and local sharing in tax support?
- Mandatory local effort?
- State responsibility for fulfillment of the foundation program?
- Tax leeway for experimental and quality programs?
- Local responsibility for educational programs?
- Periodic appraisal and revision of the state aid plan?

A state should develop a program by which the state and local districts together can utilize the financial resources available to them to support public education in the most efficient manner.

If it does nothing else, the state makes possible the financing of education by creating school districts and giving them the power to levy and collect taxes. However, since districts vary greatly in wealth, with some districts possessing insufficient tax resources to support education, practically all states provide supplementary assistance from state tax revenues.

The tax revenues available to most school districts are limited to the property tax. This is not always the most equitable means of deriving support for education. The sources tapped by state taxes provide a broadened base for school support.

Experience of the last three or four decades has provided some guidelines which are gaining acceptance in programs of financing schools. Among the guidelines are the following:

1. *A foundation program should be defined and should be expressed in dollar terms.*

The previous chapter considered means of determining the amount needed for a foundation program. It is generally thought that a foundation program should be comprehensive, including all of the elements of an educational program that the state determines should be made available to the children. There should be few special aids for particular aspects of the school program; for example, the state must decide whether kindergarten programs or community college programs sponsored by local school districts are to be part of the foundation program.

The foundation program depicts the dollar need for a minimum program of education. This need is usually represented in dollars per pupil or dollars per classroom unit. The classroom unit is related to the pupil unit in that it is basically an aggregation of pupil units with a definitely specified pupil-teacher ratio. The pupils to be counted are usually represented as the number of pupils enrolled, the number in average daily membership, the number in average daily attendance, or the number of pupils on the school census. This last measure, although still employed in several states, is not regarded as a very valid measure of the needs of the school district as it includes all children of school age in the district, regardless of whether they are in public or private schools.

Often these enrollment, membership, or attendance figures are based on data for the preceding year, so that the exact amount of state aid can be determined in advance of the year in which the aid is to be given. Some states start with data for the previous year and make adjustments as more up-to-date measures become available. One state, Michigan, has found that the number of students in membership on the fourth Friday of a school year correlates highly with average daily membership for the entire year; so Michigan bases its pupil count for state aid purposes on the fourth Friday figure. Such a procedure tends to recognize the current year's enrollment in rapidly growing school districts and gives a figure which is easy to audit or verify.

Many states use a refined version of the dollars-per-pupil figure to reflect increased costs for pupils with particularly unique needs. The cost of educating a physically handicapped student, for example, may be several times the cost of educating a student who does not need such a markedly differentiated program. This has led to the use of a weighted pupil figure as described in the previous chapter.[1]

To be satisfactory in any state a foundation program must be:

---

[1] *Supra,* p. 20.

1. Inclusive—all of the major elements of education that should be available to every child should be included in the program;
2. Cooperatively determined—lay citizens as well as professional educators should participate in making the decisions as to the nature and level of support program that the state must have;
3. Objectively determined—the dollar figure expressed in per pupil or classroom unit terms should be such that any person following the stipulated formula would arrive at the same results;
4. Easily understood so that lay citizens, including legislators, are familiar with the formula and can explain its operation.

2. *The state and the local school district should share in securing the funds to fulfill the foundation program.*

By themselves many if not most school systems possess inadequate resources to finance the foundation program. The taxing authority granted most school systems is limited to the property tax, but reasonable levies on property will not yield sufficient revenue to finance a minimum program of education in many districts. The state must take on the function of providing substantial revenues for education largely because of this lack of tax resources at the local level.

The amount of property valuation in a school district is not always directly proportional to the number of school children to be served. Some districts are overflowing with pupils, yet possess but meager tax valuations. Other districts come closer to realizing the amount needed for a foundation program with their local levy. It therefore seems equitable that the extreme fluctuations should be eliminated or at least softened by differential amounts of state assistance, with aid flowing in greater amounts to the poorer districts. Thus, through state aid many states endeavor to achieve some equalization of the tax effort demanded of each local school system in fulfillment of the foundation program.

There are those who argue that, since education is a state function, there should be some financing of the school program from the state level. They do not argue for a high degree of state control of education but for a recognition of the fact that in the last analysis the school system is a state system, that even school districts are creations of the state. Since the ultimate responsibility for education rests with the state, there should be some acceptance by the state of financial obligation.

GUIDELINES FOR STATE SCHOOL SUPPORT 31

Substantial assistance from the state has not always been the rule. Until the 1920s the large majority of the states expected school financial support to come almost exclusively from local sources. Even today, there are marked variations between the states in the extent to which they share the financial burdens of education with the local districts. Table 6 shows the relative percentages of funds derived from federal, state, and local sources for the support of education in the various states.

The marked variations between states illustrated in Table 6 raise

TABLE 6

PERCENTAGES OF REVENUE ESTIMATED FROM FEDERAL, STATE AND LOCAL SOURCES, 1965–66.*

State	Federal Sources	State Sources	Local Sources	State	Federal Sources	State Sources	Local Sources
United States, total	7.8%	39.1%	53.1%				
Alabama	15.4	60.8	23.8	Montana	8.0	27.9	64.1
Alaska	27.5	51.4	21.1	Nebraska	7.2	5.9	86.9
Arizona	13.3	36.3	50.4	Nevada	8.2	51.9	39.9
Arkansas	20.1	43.4	36.5	New Hampshire	6.1	10.7	83.2
California	6.4	38.5	55.0	New Jersey	4.5	21.2	74.4
Colorado	8.9	24.6	66.4	New Mexico	13.6	65.3	20.9
Connecticut	5.1	32.8	62.0	New York	6.0	44.2	49.8
Delaware	5.7	75.5	18.9	North Carolina	11.8	65.9	22.3
Florida	9.4	48.8	41.8	North Dakota	7.6	26.1	66.3
Georgia	12.0	61.4	26.6	Ohio	5.0	27.4	67.6
Hawaii	11.2	61.5	27.3	Oklahoma	14.1	29.4	56.6
Idaho	7.5	38.5	54.0	Oregon	7.9	26.5	65.6
Illinois	5.7	22.9	71.3	Pennsylvania	7.1	41.7	51.2
Indiana	5.7	37.1	57.3	Rhode Island	7.6	31.6	60.8
Iowa	4.7	13.5	81.8	South Carolina	17.3	59.7	23.0
Kansas	8.3	21.6	70.1	South Dakota	17.0	11.9	71.0
Kentucky	14.2	52.0	33.8	Tennessee	11.7	49.5	38.7
Louisiana	6.0	69.2	24.8	Texas	7.0	52.0	40.9
Maine	10.8	29.0	60.2	Utah	9.0	49.0	42.1
Maryland	7.3	32.0	60.6	Vermont	8.3	26.2	65.4
Massachusetts	9.6	22.1	68.3	Virginia	11.1	39.4	49.5
Michigan	6.1	43.9	50.0	Washington	6.1	58.3	35.6
Minnesota	6.5	38.0	55.6	West Virginia	7.2	52.1	40.7
Mississippi	20.0	51.0	29.1	Wisconsin	7.4	23.8	68.8
Missouri	8.5	31.8	59.7	Wyoming	6.3	42.0	51.7

* Data from *Estimates of School Statistics, 1965–66*, Research Report 1965-R17. Washington: National Education Association, 1965. Table 10, p. 32. Because of rounding, the percent distribution may not add exactly to 100%.

a question as to whether there has always been joint planning between states and local school districts in determining the relative commitments to be made in providing at least a floor level of educational opportunity. In some states planning has been haphazard. There has not always been a commitment to provide adequate financing for a foundation program of education. The yields of existing taxes, rather than the needs of a foundation program, have frequently been the point of departure for school support. This fact leads to the next two guidelines.

3. *The ability of a local school district to contribute to the dollar amount required in the foundation formula must be determined, and there must be a mandatory local effort.*

If a partnership is to succeed, each partner must put forth reasonable effort. One must decide how the capability of a school district to meet its share of financing the schools can be determined.

At the local level, the traditional source of taxable wealth is the value of property. It could be expected, then, that one measure which might be used is the amount of dollars per pupil that a specified millage rate would yield when applied to the total value of the property in the school district. The specified millage rate, which would be set by the state, should be high enough so that substantial effort would be made by the district for the support of education, yet low enough so that total taxes would not be confiscatory and so that some margin would be left to meet the varying and unusual needs of school districts. Educational experimentation could be provided for by keeping the millage rate low enough to allow the possibility of additional local tax levies above those mandated by the state.

The amount of dollars per pupil raised by a stipulated millage rate on property valuation is the measure of ability used by most states. It has some drawbacks. The value of property may no longer be the best measure of the wealth of an individual, the aggregate value of property in a school district no longer the best measure of the wealth of a school district. Wealth may be represented in such intangibles as stocks and bonds rather than in real estate. Then there is the problem of determining the value of the property. This has traditionally been done by a local assessor's estimating the worth of the property and entering its "assessed value" on the tax rolls. The assessed value is rarely the true market value of the property. Some assessors more nearly approach the true value than others. The Committee on Tax Education and School Finance of the National Education Association points out:

> Some local assessors have kept their valuations low in order to qualify their districts for more state aid or to minimize the burden of a state property tax on taxpayers within their districts. In states where the county or township assessor can manipulate assessments to make his district look poor by assessing at a fraction of full value, assessment rolls lose their validity as measures of fiscal capacity for the distribution of state school funds.[2]

Some states have sought to develop tax manuals for assessors, spelling out the yardsticks to be used, and have in addition provided some supervision of the work of local assessors. Nearly half of the states now use formulas applied at the state level to arrive at "equalized valuations" which are then used in determining the ability of a school district to support the local share of educational costs.

A number of the states, located mostly in the southeast section of the United States, have experimented with the use of an index comprising economic factors as a means of measuring the ability of a local school district to support education. Such factors as these have been included in one or more of the indices: retail sales tax receipts; personal income as measured by payroll data or income tax payments; value of farming, manufacturing, and mining production; automobile vehicle registrations or automobile license tax paid; postal receipts. Measures on the various factors in the index are compiled for each school district. It is determined what portion of the total wealth of the state each district possesses on each of these factors. A combined index is then derived, with some of the factors sometimes weighted more heavily than others, representing the portion of the wealth of the state possessed by a school district as measured by the factors in the index. The school district is then expected to tax itself to provide that proportion of the total amount of school revenue to be raised in the state through local tax levies. This dollar amount usually has to be translated into a millage rate for each district and applied against the property valuation in the district. The use of an economic index does not by itself allocate

---

[2] Committee on Tax Education and School Finance, National Education Association, *Equalization of Property Assessments*. Washington: National Education Association, 1958, p. 7.

any additional tax resources to the district, so the usual source of property tax revenue must still be tapped. The millages levied will vary between districts, being adjusted to raise the amount of money required by the application of the index of economic factors.

The problem of calculating wealth on a series of economic factors but then still levying taxes on the real estate valuations which were shunned as a fair measure of wealth causes Corbally to comment:

> If local school financial support is derived from property taxation, then measures of the property tax seem the only valid measures of the local ability to support schools.[3]

In some instances, the local assessed valuations are included as one of the factors in the economic index. In at least one state, the economic index is averaged equally with the total assessed valuation in the district to determine the portion of the total local school revenues of the state a given district should be required to raise.

The economic index has the advantage of objectivity. Data on the various economic factors are not so subject to local manipulation as are property assessments. On the other hand, it is usually very difficult to obtain data by school districts for economic factors which presumably measure school district wealth as the statistics for these factors are not usually available below the county level. Most of the states which have employed an economic index use counties as the basic unit of school administration.

Prior to World War II only one state, Alabama, had used an economic index to measure the ability of school districts to support education; since World War II a half dozen states have employed some form of an economic index. This "trend" seems to be slackening, however. The consensus among authorities seems to be that reforms in property taxation that will provide valid assessments are essential since revenues for local school support will continue to be drawn largely from the property source. If reforms are made in property tax administration, a specified millage measure applied to property valuation seems the most usable single index of the financial capacity of the local school system.

4. *The state must provide at least the difference between the amount raised by the mandatory local tax effort and the total dollar*

---

[3] John E. Corbally, Jr., *School Finance*. Boston: Allyn and Bacon, Inc., 1962, pp. 110–11.

amount required for the foundation program for the school district.

Throughout the United States, more than ten billion dollars in state funds are distributed annually to local school districts—a figure which represents about 40 per cent of the total costs of public elementary and secondary school education in the United States. As has been shown in Table 6, however, there are marked variations between the states in the percentage of school costs derived from revenues collected at the state level.

The violation of this fourth principle, that the state must provide the difference between the uniform local tax effort and the amount of funds required by the foundation program, constitutes one of the major problems in school finance. Legislatures have not always provided sufficient appropriations at the state level to cover the state's share of the foundation program. Sometimes funds are pro-rated to provide for fulfillment of only a fractional share of the foundation program. The state may, for example, assume only eighty per cent of its obligation, rationalizing that this is all that existing revenue measures can provide. When this happens the idea of a foundation program is entirely vitiated. The minimum educational program goes out the window, being replaced by a dollar amount bearing no relation to justified educational need. Moreover, it is the poorer districts which suffer most when percentage adjustments are made. A rich district can make a slight extra local millage levy above the mandatory tax level and realize the foundation amount. A poor district would have to raise many times the extra millage of the rich district to realize the foundation amount. This principle, sometimes called the principle of "adequacy," stresses the fact that the state-local partnership demands a sufficiency of funds to meet the foundation program which the state has agreed to support.

While local school revenues are limited largely to the property tax in most states, legislatures which decide the sources of state revenue measures have many tax sources which may be tapped, limited only by stipulations written into state constitutions. In most states major appropriations for education are commonly made from the general treasury of the state rather than from specific tax sources earmarked for education. There are exceptions to this, particularly in instances in which revenue from land grants given by the federal government to the states for educational purposes decree an ear-

36   GUIDELINES FOR STATE SCHOOL SUPPORT

marked revenue measure. The point that is being stressed is that the state government has more latitude in determining the nature and amount of taxes than do local school districts which in most instances are dependent on the property tax. With the flexibility in revenue measures provided state legislatures, the state is in a better position than the local district to guarantee that the full amount needed for the foundation program is raised.

Table 7 illustrates how local and state shares might be determined in a foundation program which requires $500 per pupil to provide the minimum education program which the state and local school district together agree to underwrite.

TABLE 7

LOCAL AND STATE SHARE IN A FOUNDATION PROGRAM REQUIRING $500 PER PUPIL WITH A 12 MILL MANDATORY LOCAL DISTRICT LEVY*

Valuation per pupil in the school district	Local share provided by a 12 mill levy	State share to provide remainder needed above local levy
$36,000	$432	$ 68
33,000	396	104
30,000	360	140
27,000	324	176
24,000	288	212
21,000	252	248
18,000	216	284
15,000	180	320
12,000	144	356
9,000	108	392
6,000	72	428

* In this table, the entire state aid is distributed on an equalization basis. In most states, all school districts receive some flat grants apart from equalization funds; so this table represents an oversimplification to illustrate a point. A more typical state aid pattern is shown in Figure 3, *infra*, p. 47.

5. *Local school districts should be encouraged to tax themselves beyond the mandatory local tax effort required in the foundation program in order to provide educational opportunities beyond the foundation program.*

The foundation program was defined as the minimum program of education which should be available to all pupils in the state. Achievement of the foundation program may wipe out educational deprivation, but it does not provide for the continued forward thrust of education that must come through educational innovation and experimentation, from programs that strive for high quality rather than minimum conformity.

This fifth principle is the principle of local "tax leeway." Morphet describes it as follows:

> There should be provision for the citizens of each local school system, without handicapping restrictions, to vote and levy on themselves any taxes they consider desirable and necessary to provide additional or better educational services and facilities than those provided through the foundation program.[4]

The setting of the local mandatory tax levy which operates to provide funds for the foundation program is the first key to the successful operation of this principle. This mandatory tax levy must not be set so high that it exhausts the possibility of additional local effort. There must be "leeway" so that a district may exert itself to provide an educational program that goes beyond the foundation program.

At present, the major motivation for a district's taxing itself an additional amount over that provided by the mandatory levy is the desire of the people to have an educational program above the foundation level. There is increasing discussion of more tangible encouragement to school districts with some form of matching state aid for levies beyond the mandatory rate. The argument is that if one partner in the state-local sharing is willing to make more effort to improve educational programs, shouldn't the other partner likewise make extra effort? To date the resources of most states have been channeled toward realization of foundation programs. In the years ahead the question of incentives for quality will receive much consideration.

6. *The state plan of financing schools should encourage local responsibility for school administration and should avoid specific controls enforced through the finance plan.*

The state undoubtedly must define and enforce certain minimum requirements to which school districts must conform. It is not unreasonable to require that a school district provide a minimum

---

[4] Edgar L. Morphet, "Developing Sound Foundation Programs," *Problems and Opportunities in Financing Education, Proceedings of the Second National Conference on School Finance Problems, 1959.* Washington: National Education Association, 1959, p. 117.

number of school days of instruction a year and the need for teacher certification standards has been amply demonstrated. But few of these controls should be enforced primarily through the finance plan. The withholding of state aid is, of course, an effective sanction against a school district unwilling to assume responsibility for an adequate educational program. But this sanction should be used sparingly and only in connection with absolutely minimum requirements. The threat of rigid, standardized controls is a much greater threat than the failure of a few school systems to provide minimum educational opportunities, particularly if the financial means have been made available to the local school system through a foundation program.

There is widespread agreement that the upgrading of education by the state is better accomplished through the leadership and service activities of the staff of the state department of education than it is through a multiplicity of restrictive requirements. Statutes and regulations designed to force a district with an inadequate program either to achieve a minimum program or to lose state aid sometimes become rigid and inflexible to the extent of restricting the pioneering district from introducing unusual patterns of instruction or administration. The compelling necessity for a minimum requirement to be enforced through the state aid act must be firmly established.

The focus of state finance plans should be on the encouragement of local leadership and responsibility. The district with inadequate financing has few choices that can be made. It will be forced to employ the least qualified teachers at the lowest salary rates and to have a high pupil-teacher ratio. But if a state financing program is adequate to provide a foundation program and still permit latitude for extra local millage levies for high quality programs and for experimental patterns, the board of education of the local district is in a position to make choices, to determine priorities, to exercise the local leadership and control which are the hallmarks of American public elementary and secondary education.

7. *There should be periodic evaluation and modification of the state finance plan in the light of experience and in response to emerging educational needs.*

The dollar amount per pupil or per classroom unit to be provided in a foundation program may be derived in different ways as outlined in the previous chapter. The method of linking the foundation amount to the salary required to secure a qualified beginning teacher or to the average salary paid teachers in an intermediate unit or in a state contains a built-in provision for adjusting the foundation figure as instructional costs increase. The method of pricing the various services defined as being in the foundation program contains no such provision for adjustment except as these costs are periodically assessed. Then, too, notions of what constitutes "minimum services" are subject to revision. As experimental programs prove their worth they may be incorporated in the foundation program. As the Committee on Tax Education and School Finance of the National Education Association points out, "The expenditure level should be viewed as transitory and subject to increase as new concepts and desires of the people in a state develop."[5]

---

[5] Committee on Tax Education and School Finance, National Education Association, *Guides to the Improvement of State School Finance Programs*. Washington: National Education Association, 1958, p. 22.

CHAPTER IV

Issues and Problems in the Administration of State Support

What considerations underlie the following issues in state school finance?

- A comprehensive program vs. special aids.
- Flat grants vs. equalization aid.
- Local responsibility for utilizing tax leeway vs. incentive aid.
- State aid for educational improvement vs. state aid for tax relief.
- Objective administration by formula vs. provisions for a contingency fund.
- Separation of church and state in educational financing vs. tax support of non-public schools.

Issues Underlying a State Plan for Financing Education

Some of the issues have been implied in the discussion of the characteristics of a state plan. Other issues arise as state officials seek to place a state plan in operation. Among the issues which must be resolved in any state plan are these:

1. *Should there be a single all-embracing foundation program or are special aid funds for certain types of expenditures warranted?*

Prevailing opinion among writers and researchers in the field of educational finance is that the foundation program should be comprehensive. The essential elements which should be available to all pupils should be included in it. From time to time, however, states have sought to stimulate certain types of programs by providing special aid, often on a matching basis, to those school districts which agree to undertake the programs specified. In this fashion encouragement has been given the development of vocational programs, the establishment of school libraries, provision for special programs for the physically and mentally handicapped, visiting teacher programs, driver education, and a host of other programs to which the state wishes to give particular encouragement.

There are several objections to state programs which incorporate a substantial number of special aids. Once the value of a program has been established, it should be made available to all children by being incorporated in the foundation program. Then, too, a board of education confronted with funds provided by the state for some activities and not for others may abdicate its responsibility for determining the priority of elements in a curricular program and commit funds to match those being provided by the state.

> When used excessively, it is possible for special aids to have a restrictive effect upon local budgets and adaptability. Since such special aids substitute central direction for local initiative, they sometimes distort local budgets and thereby impede adaptability and school quality.[1]

Special aids which require matching are more easily incorporated in the programs of the wealthier districts than in those of the poorer districts. Where property valuation is high a small increase in millage will provide the matching funds needed to obtain a state grant, but a poor district may find substantial millage increases required to raise the funds needed to qualify for matching grants.

If stimulative grants are used to encourage the inauguration of desirable new curricular programs, they should be provided for a limited period of years with the provision that the school district will incorporate the cost of the program as part of the regular school budget if it has proved its worth after a trial period.

The trend is toward fewer special aids. In a study of educational finance which involved thirty-six states, however, Strayer found that among the special purpose grants in existence, the range of years that they had been in effect varied from two to thirty-seven years continuously.[2]

Some special aids continue in existence because they represent needs which are not felt equally in all school districts. It is difficult to incorporate an amount in a foundation formula which takes care

---

[1] Committee on Tax Education and School Finance, National Education Association, *Guides to the Improvement of State School Finance Programs*. Washington: National Education Association, 1958, p. 20.

[2] George D. Strayer, Jr., *Guidelines for Public School Finance*. Bloomington, Indiana: Phi Delta Kappa, 1963, p. 13.

of variations between districts equitably. Transportation of pupils is a case in point. The cost of transporting pupils may vary from no cost in an urban area to nearly a hundred dollars per pupil annually in a rural area. Similarly, the costs of new school construction carry varying impacts on school districts. Rapidly expanding suburban districts may find a disproportionate amount of their educational budget flowing into new physical facilities.

Some special aids cannot be incorporated in the foundation amount because they involve federal funds channeled through the state department of education for particular purposes. They must be used for the purpose intended and there must be accountability of expenditures. The programs in aid of vocational education and the hot lunch program are examples.

Some states recognize that thinly settled rural areas have unique problems. A more heavily weighted pupil unit or classroom unit is sometimes allowed such areas in the foundation formula. This may be one way of incorporating the unusual pupil transportation problem in the foundation formula, but it also recognizes that the usual class size cannot be maintained in small rural schools. A one room school of twelve students does not derive a sufficient amount of support if aid is based on a per pupil unit. Advanced high school classes in mathematics, languages, and the sciences are likely to have few pupils in them, but they need to be offered if able rural students are to have educational opportunities available to them. Such an adjustment for rural communities in the state aid formula is called a sparsity correction. There is danger, of course, that in some cases when this correction is allowed aid may be given inefficient school districts which ought to reorganize into larger districts.

Within the last five years, representations have been made by large urban school districts requesting that their problems be given special consideration either by a weighted per pupil or weighted classroom index or else by out and out special aid. These districts point out that education must share the tax dollar with other governmental services to a greater extent than is true in suburban, small city, or rural areas. In addition, the value of real property has declined in many metropolitan centers or the advance in property valuation has not kept pace with the pupil needs which must be met. This decline in valuation is due in part to property deteriora-

ISSUES AND PROBLEMS 43

tion as homeowners move to suburban areas and their old homes become rental units. Furthermore, there is a removal of property valuation from the tax rolls because of freeway projects and property taken for public housing which does not immediately yield the income formerly derived from taxation. All this is accompanied by a wave of in-migrant children a disproportionate number of whom have low motivation, require remedial help, are early drop-outs, swell the ranks of delinquents, and need reorientation and specific job and citizenship training.

> The situation constitutes a grave educational problem and an added financial burden as the schools try to meet the needs of these people who require an increasingly larger share of special services offered by counselors, social service workers, attendance officers, psychologists, doctors, nurses, psychiatrists, and others.[3]

In only a few instances have the problems of the metropolis been recognized in terms of financial assistance:

> Except for a recent (1962) New York State school support program, States generally have not recognized that the per pupil expenses in city school systems are greater than the average. Nor have they taken into account the fact that vocational education is more expensive per pupil than are the usual nonvocational programs. Even though the city schools provide expensive special and vocational education (at a relatively higher cost per pupil than is often experienced in rural and suburban areas) their State per pupil reimbursement may be no higher than or not as high as that provided to rural and suburban schools.[4]

As the troops are mustered for the war on poverty, financial assistance for the metropolitan schools is likely to be an accompanying development. If corrections can be made for "sparsity," perhaps corrections are equally warranted for the densely congested area with its different but even more overwhelming problems.

2. *To what extent should state aid be allocated on the basis of flat grants and to what extent should state aid be allocated on an equalization basis?*

A flat grant allocation or a general aid is an identical per pupil

---

[3] "The Impact of Urbanization on Education," *Summary Report of a Conference, May 23–29, 1962*. Washington: U.S. Department of Health, Education and Welfare, Office of Education, 1962, p. 6. Superintendent of Documents Catalog No. FS 5.210:10021.

[4] *Ibid.*, p. 10.

dollar amount given by the state to all school districts regardless of wealth. Equalization aid is the dollar amount of aid necessary to enable a district to reach the foundation program after it has made the reasonable local effort required by the mandatory levy and after any flat grants received are added to the required local effort.

Equalization aid is an absolute essential if the children in all districts are to have at least a minimum educational opportunity. Most authorities in the field of educational finance contend that the bulk of state funds should be distributed on an equalization basis.

Still, there are arguments for some flat grant or general aid. Because education is a state responsibility a portion of the taxes necessary to carry out that responsibility is fairly chargeable against state funds. The flat grant pattern is a means of broadening the tax base for the support of education. Most districts are limited to the property tax for local revenues, but all of their citizens have state taxes for state functions levied against them. A return of some of the revenue raised through state taxes for local school purposes has the effect of broadening the tax base available for education. Rosenstengel and Eastmond contend that "it is a desirable way of returning to localities the revenue from equitable taxes that because of their nature cannot be efficiently administered on the local level."[5] In effect, local non-property resources are made available to local school districts through the state's power to tax.

The Committee on Tax Education and School Finance of the National Education Association states in a 1958 publication that "the extension of support to all local school districts regardless of taxpaying ability not only develops a sense of broader responsibility but also creates tax leeway for the exercise of local initiative."[6]

A general subvention to rich districts as well as to poor districts is sometimes justified on the ground that the wealthy district which can underwrite a foundation program by its own efforts can use the extra funds derived from the state for experimental purposes, thus contributing to the advance of education. Their schools can

---

[5] William Everett Rosenstengel and Jefferson N. Eastmond, *School Finance.* New York: The Ronald Press, 1957, pp. 89–90.

[6] Committee on Tax Education and School Finance, National Education Association, *Guides to the Improvement of State School Finance Programs.* Washington: National Education Association, 1958, p. 15.

become pilot or "lighthouse" schools with the results of their experimentation being made available to all schools and some of their innovations becoming incorporated in a revised foundation program. This argument, although frequently advanced, seems somewhat specious. Should these opportunities for experimentation be confined to the wealthy districts? This use of general aid is a device which singles out wealthy districts for special privilege.

It is often pointed out that general aid does have an equalizing influence for it is combined with local tax effort to more nearly approach the amount of dollars necessary to fund the foundation program. Moreover, there is an equalizing influence in the sources of revenue from which general aid is secured: the wealthy districts will have contributed far more in income, sales, and other state taxes than they receive back in aid to schools. Thus tax income, which is derived on the basis of wealth, is distributed either on a flat grant basis in which all share equally or on an equalization basis in which poorer districts share to an even greater extent. The equalization that occurs on the income side of the ledger is frequently overlooked as state plans for the support of education are developed.

Flat grants have an advantage over equalization funds in that they are easily understood and easily administered. The concept of the state's providing the same amount to each pupil or to each classroom unit in a district is not hard to grasp and the data for administering the grant is quickly, easily, and objectively determined. State assistance primarily on the basis of equalization is opposed in some quarters on the grounds that local fair effort is not accurately determined by the mandatory millage yardstick and that equalization funds flow in greater measure to districts which have managed to keep their property valuations depressed. Equalization funds will continue to be resisted in these quarters until there is more objective assessment of property with the property in all districts being equitably treated.

Flat grants are sometimes incorporated in state aid plans on practical rather than on theoretical grounds. It is difficult to pass legislation which provides state assistance to some districts and not to others. Legislators from even the wealthy districts seem to desire that the districts they represent receive some state assistance as part of a state aid bill. In most states there are few districts with valuations which yield the foundation amount on the basis of local levies alone; but to encourage the favorable votes of legislators from these districts, an arbitrary per pupil general aid is sometimes incorporated in the state aid formula.

In many state aid formulas equalization aid is applied on top of general aid—the amount of the equalization aid being the dollars necessary to reach the foundation amount after dollars raised locally by the mandatory levy and dollars provided in the general aid are added together. General aid, then, assists in the equalization function except in those wealthy districts in which equalization aid is not necessary. The great danger in flat or general grants is that they divert funds that are needed for equalization in order to maintain a foundation program. Corbally points out:

> If the total amount of state revenue available for the support of public schools is somewhat fixed, it is apparent that the more dollars that are used for flat grant purposes, the less will be available for equalization purposes. As the amount for equalization purposes is reduced, the guaranteed minimum revenue per pupil for the neediest districts will also have to be reduced. The equalization effect will then be reduced and sharp differences in revenue per pupil will exist even when needy districts make more local effort than do the wealthy districts.[7]

Figure 3 portrays a state aid plan operating under the concept of a foundation program and combining both general and equalization aid. The fabric of many state aid plans is similar to that illustrated in Figure 3. While the financing of only eleven districts is portrayed, these districts cover the spectrum of a typical state aid program. The following points can be noted:

1. All districts have sufficient funds to underwrite the foundation program.
2. The general or flat grant aid is constant; the same per pupil amount is received by every school district.
3. The amount of equalization aid varies greatly, depending on what is required to realize the foundation program. In District K 80 per cent of the dollars required for a minimum educational program are provided by the state. More than half of this is in equalization aid. At the other extreme Districts A and B receive no equalization aid.

---

[7] John E. Corbally, Jr., *School Finance*. Boston: Allyn and Bacon, Inc., 1962, p. 130.

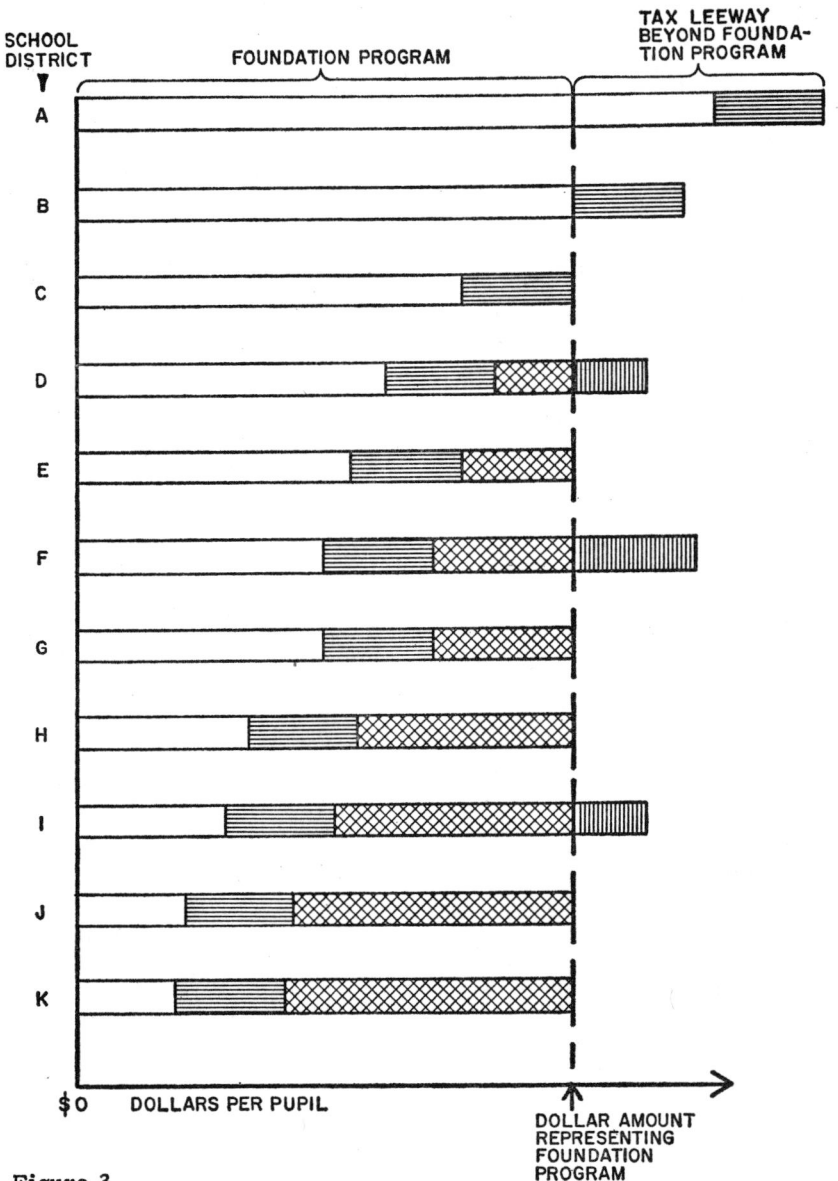

Figure 3.
Source of Funds for the Support of Education in Eleven School Districts in a Typical State Foundation Program with Mandatory Local Effort and with both General Aid and Equalization Funds.

CODE: DOLLARS PER PUPIL ACCRUING FROM:
LOCAL MANDATORY LEVEL   GENERAL OR FLAT GRANT AID   EQUALIZATION FUNDS   ADDITIONAL OPTIONAL LOCAL LEVY

4. The mandatory local levy in District A yields more revenue than is required for the foundation program. District A still receives some state aid, however, as it is eligible for general or flat grant aid.
5. Three districts (D, F, and I) have chosen to impose extra millage levies at the local level in order to undertake innovations requiring extra funds or to build toward quality programs. Although District I raises the same per pupil dollar amount beyond the foundation program as District D, the extra millage levy in District I will be twice as high as in District D because of the lower property valuation in District I.

3. Should additional local effort beyond the local mandatory levy be matched by additional state funds beyond those required to realize the foundation program?

The concept of tax leeway which permits a local school district to levy additional local taxes to provide better educational opportunities than the minimum assured in the foundation program constituted the fifth characteristic of a state plan discussed in the last chapter. There is universal agreement that the mandatory millage required should not be so high that communities are not motivated to make additional local effort to secure a better educational program than provided by the "floor" of the state plan. But should the state reward those communities which do exert extra effort because the state likewise has a stake in quality programs and in innovation and experimentation? And if it does reward them, on what basis?

In the 1962 conference on school finance sponsored by the Committee on Tax Education and School Finance of the National Education Association, James predicts:

> I suspect we are nearing the end of half a century of emphasis on equalization, and that a trend has begun, and will be extended toward state encouragement to local communities which put forth additional effort to provide good educational programs. The states will guarantee minimum programs, through machinery comparable to the foundation program as we now know it, but will begin to devise partnership arrangements for sharing the costs with those districts which choose to go beyond the mandated program in the pursuit of excellence.[8]

---

[8] H. Thomas James, "New Developments in State School Finance," *Financing the Changing School Program,* Proceedings of the Fifth National School Finance Conference. Washington: National Education Association, 1962, p. 89.

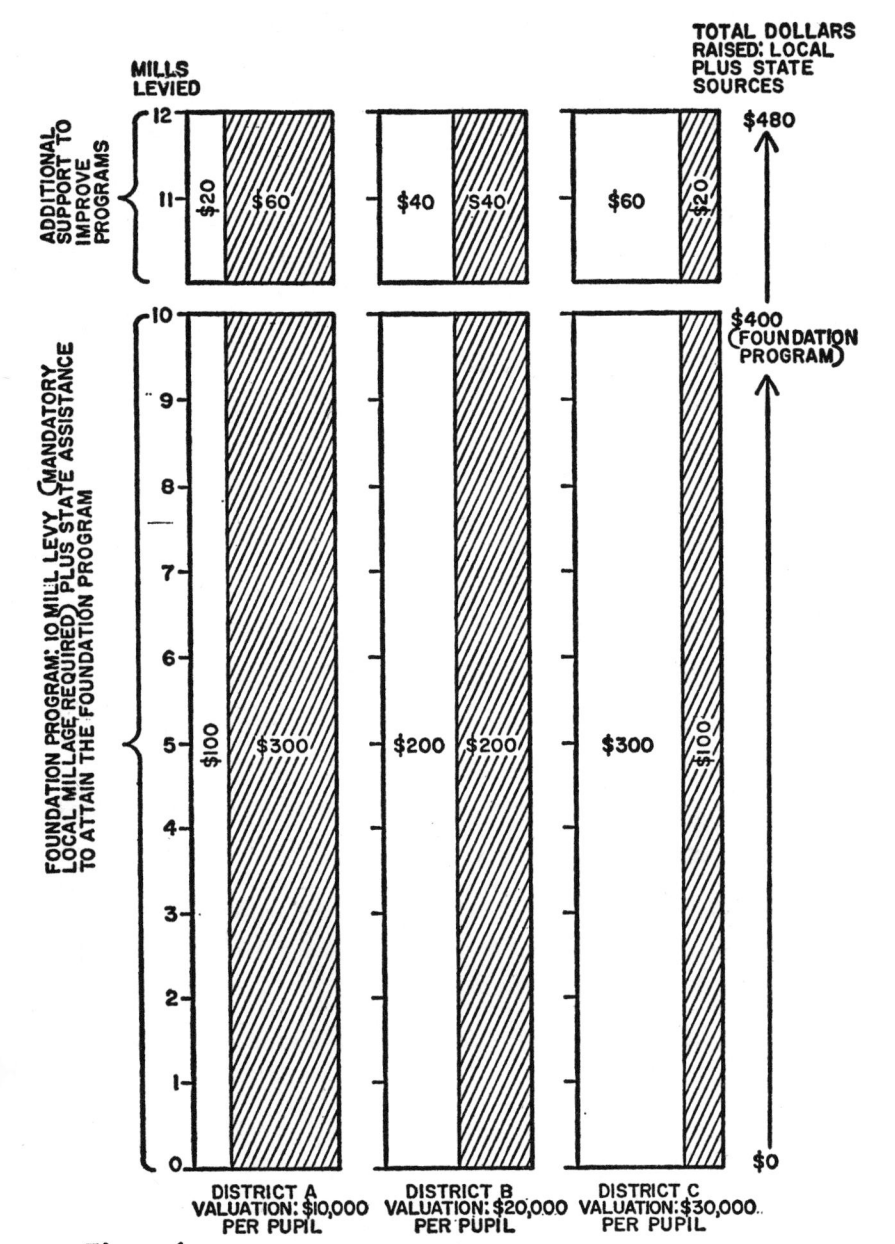

Figure 4.
Graphic Presentation of a State Aid Plan whereby Districts of Varying Wealth Support the Same Level of Expenditure Per Pupil when There is Identical Local Tax Effort.

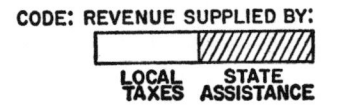

In order to spur movement toward quality programs states may provide an extra per pupil dollar amount above the foundation figure for every mill levied by a school district above the mandatory millage. This represents a flat grant to promote incentive effort above a minimum program. Some states seek to have equalization operate at this level as well as in the foundation program. Equal effort would result in an equal dollar amount expended per pupil regardless of the wealth of the school district. A financial plan of this character is illustrated in Figure 4. The mandatory millage in this graph is arbitrarily set at ten mills, but the scheme would operate with any other specified mandatory millage. In all three districts, an extra two mill levy above the mandatory level results in an additional $80 per pupil being available for the schools' operations. Funds from the state supplement each additional mill levied so that every district has the same dollar amount to spend per pupil for each mill levied.

The New York State Educational Conference Board has proposed a plan somewhat similar to this. It goes so far as to abolish the foundation program concept and to relate state aid directly to local effort at whatever level that local effort may be pegged:

> The Board proposed state equalization of local taxation, accomplished by establishing a sliding scale of percentages of state support according to the taxable wealth of a locality, and applying these percentages to the locally adopted school budgets. The only control on local spending proposed was a limit on the annual increase in the budgets subject to state sharing—$50 per pupil unit for current expenditures. Under this proposal a poor district, an average district, or a district with above average wealth all could support the same level of expenditure per pupil unit with a given local tax effort.[9]

Wisconsin, Rhode Island, and Maryland are states which reward extra millage effort by providing incentive assistance in the state aid program.

4. *Should the objective of the state support program be to equalize and improve educational opportunities or to afford relief to local property taxes?*

This issue may be falsely stated—a true dichotomy may not be

---

[9] Arvid J. Burke, "A Dynamic Finance Policy," *Financing the Changing School Program,* Proceedings of the Fifth National School Finance Conference. Washington: National Education Association, 1962, pp. 83–84.

ISSUES AND PROBLEMS 51

presented. Certainly the first objective of a state support program is to provide at least a minimum program for all children; and if a choice has to be made between educational opportunity and high property tax levies, the choice had better be made in favor of educational opportunity. But the decision is not this simple. Excessive property tax levies, particularly on industrial property, will discourage the development and expansion of productive enterprise in the state, curtailing the tax base on which further school levies depend.

There are many pressures for property tax relief. Levies have reached unreasonably excessive heights in some local communities. It is possible for legislation to be passed providing substantial increases in state aid funds for the purpose of affording local tax relief. It is also possible that the goal of increased state aid may be to guarantee that the foundation program is financed fully or to provide incentive funds for quality programs. Sometimes these goals merge, but when they do there should be clarity as to the proportions of increased state aid designed for each purpose.

James presents the problem in this fashion:

> The first and most fundamental distinction to be made among state plans for distributing funds to local school districts is therefore between those plans directed to the support of educational services, and those plans directed to the relief of local property tax burdens. Much of the obscurity of typical discussions of school finance, and most of the complexities in school finance plans and their statutory descriptions, arise out of failure to distinguish these two purposes, as well as out of deliberate attempts in many instances to convey an impression of accomplishing both purposes at once.[10]

What perturbs James is that both purposes are often represented as being the goals of state aid legislation, but when the final appropriations are voted at the concluding legislative session, the appropriations are lower than the requested assistance. Taxes may be shifted from one base to another but the total revenues for schools may not be increased substantially.

5. *Should a state contingency fund be available for allocation to distressed school districts in emergencies and catastrophes?*

As a general rule, the funds distributed by the state to local

---

[10] H. Thomas James, "Financing Elementary and Secondary Education," text of an address delivered at the Midwestern Regional Conference of the Council of State Governments, Davenport, Iowa, July 23, 1963, p. 1.

school districts should be subject to formula and capable of objective determination. A taxpayer, a local superintendent, and an official of the state department of public instruction should all arrive at the same answer when computing the state aid to which a district is entitled. When major catastrophes occur, however, such as a fire, a flood, an earthquake, or a sudden and overwhelming increase in enrollment in cases where state aid is based on last year's average daily membership, should the chief state school officer or the state board of education have available an emergency fund which can be allocated on an individual grant basis?

Nearly half of the states have a small fund of this character authorized and appropriated along with the state aid bill. In its pamphlet, *Guidelines for Public School Finance,* the National Advisory Committee on School Finance of Phi Delta Kappa states as one guideline that "a small state contingency fund should be available for allocation under controlled conditions in case of emergencies."[11]

The discretionary judgment involved in responding to pleas for assistance is not easily exercised. Most chief state school officers dislike administration of any funds on a personal basis. Authorizing school districts to carry insurance against major catastrophes or providing statewide self-insurance programs seem better answers to the contingency fund problem.

6. *Should tax funds be used to support non-public schools?*

At the beginning of the century only one out of twenty students in elementary or secondary schools attended parochial schools. Today one out of seven is enrolled in a parochial school. The question keeps recurring as to whether tax funds can be used for any educational functions of the private or parochial school.

The issue has a constitutional setting. The first part of the First Amendment to the federal Constitution states:

> Congress shall make no law respecting an establishment of religion, or prohibiting the free exercise thereof. . . .

Nearly all states have a similar constitutional provision in their state constitutions.

Legal interpretations in case law seem to preclude direct use of tax funds to benefit any private educational program. The major

---

[11] George D. Strayer, Jr., *Guidelines for Public School Finance.* Bloomington, Indiana: Phi Delta Kappa, 1963, p. 11.

ISSUES AND PROBLEMS

borderline area revolves around a child-benefit theory in which it is contended that such services as pupil transportation, school health services, and school lunch programs are not an aid to an educational institution as such but are rather services to children, having no direct bearing on the particular instructional program of a school. These services apparently do not contravene the First Amendment to the Constitution. At least in the case of pupil transportation, the U.S. Supreme Court has held that transportation of parochial school students by public school buses does not violate the provisions of the First Amendment.[12] In a number of states, however, the highest court in the state has ruled that bus transportation of parochial school pupils violates the state's constitutional provision of separation of church and state and has enjoined the use of public school buses by private school pupils. This matter is a political and legal issue in several states at the present time.

An arrangement called shared-time, or dual registration, or part-time enrollment is being practiced by at least 280 school systems scattered throughout thirty-five states.[13] It is an issue now being placed before every school district as shared-time programs are being proposed under Titles I and III of the Elementary and Secondary Education Act. Under this plan, students attend the public school for part of the school day, taking such subjects as mathematics, science, physical education, industrial arts, and home economics. For the remainder of the school day, they attend the church-related school for such subjects as English, social studies, religious history and doctrine. Theodore Powell, a leading advocate of this plan, contends that "any child is entitled to part of the services of the public school as well as to all of them."[14]

Advantages attributed to this plan include making available to parochial school students a broader curriculum, while at the same time providing that subjects which can be related to religious concepts are taught in a church-related setting. The church-related school is relieved of providing the most expensive physical facilities —including gymnasia and laboratories—and twice as many pupils

---

[12] *Everson v. Board of Education,* 330 U.S. 1 (1947).

[13] Research Division, National Education Association, "Shared-Time Programs: An Exploratory Study," *Research Report 1964–R 10.* Washington: National Education Association, 1964, p. 7.

[14] Theodore Powell, Address given at institute of "Religion and the Schools," Purdue University, October 6–9, 1963.

can be accommodated in the course of a school day if parochial school students attend the parochial school a half day or less. The mixing of all children in the public school at least some time during the school day is said to discourage stratification into social and religious groups, providing a pluralistic environment. A feeling of cooperation is engendered between public and private schools which may be reflected in better support for public school expenditures, including bond levies for building expansion.

Those who argue against shared-time programs question the legality of providing public school facilities and teaching services to private school pupils. They dislike the expansion of the number of parochial schools which they are convinced this plan encourages, believing that democratic unity is promoted in a comprehensive school with a pupil body unsegregated by class, race, or religion. Instead of integration being realized through part-time attendance, it is argued that blocs based on religious lines, rather than integration are encouraged. If there is participation in extracurricular activities, will there be pressures to elect a Lutheran senior class president, a Baptist football captain, a Catholic student council president? If extracurricular activities are not open to students from the denominational schools, do they become second-class citizens in the public schools? What happens to students who do not elect to take part in the specialized programs of any of the church schools? Will they be stigmatized in any way? Furthermore, there are problems of scheduling, of pupil transportation between schools, of responsibility for discipline, of consistency of grading practices, and of the school calendar with respect to the observance of religious holidays.

It is not the purpose of this discussion to weigh these arguments but to point out that this is a highly controversial question with important implications for the financing of schools. In many communities there will be increased local public school costs if public schools are requested or required to provide the services called for in shared-time programs. What about state aid? Can the part-time students from the private schools be added together into full-time equivalents and state aid secured for these students? In at least two states, Michigan and Illinois, this is being done. In several other states it is not legal for part-time students to be included in the state aid count.

ISSUES AND PROBLEMS

An even greater financial question is posed by some church leaders who contend that state and federal aid should be made available to parochial and public schools alike. The premises are:

1. The state recognizes the right of the parent to send his child to a private or parochial school.
2. Attendance at a parochial school is accepted as a reasonable equivalency to attendance at a public school. Compulsory attendance laws recognize this. The citizenship preparation that the state requires for its functioning and perpetuation is accomplished in parochial schools.
3. Since the state accepts the parochial school program as a reasonable equivalency and since parochial schools perform a service in behalf of society that the public schools would otherwise have to render, parochial schools should receive public assistance on the same basis as public schools.

Sometimes the point is made on the grounds of equality of educational opportunity. Parochial school costs are mounting as are public school costs, and parochial school tuition charges are increasing. It is contended that equality of educational opportunity is not available when a parochial school parent has insufficient funds to pay the rising tuition costs on top of the taxes he has already paid for the support of public schools. Under these circumstances, he has no freedom of choice; he can only send his child to the public school. He does not have "free exercise" of religion. McClusky summarizes this view:

> The courts have made it clear that the government must leave parents free to send their children to schools of their choice. The corollary question is now before us: Does the First Amendment permit the government to respect that freedom further by arranging distribution of its various benefits so as to avoid discrimination against parents or students who make this choice?[15]

> At present, these citizen-parents do not enjoy full freedom to direct the education of their offspring, but are forced to pay a price to implement the theoretical right that is theirs.[16]

The Supreme Court has stated that neither a state nor a federal government "can pass laws which aid one religion, aid all religions,

---

[15] Neil G. McClusky, "Public Funds for Parochial Schools? Yes!" *Teachers College Record,* LXII (October 1960), 52.
[16] *Ibid.,* p. 53.

or prefer one religion over another."[17] In the recent Bible reading case, a part of Mr. Justice Rutledge's dissent in the Everson case was quoted in defining the purpose of the First Amendment:

> ... to create a complete and permanent separation of the spheres of religious activity and civil authority by comprehensively forbidding every form of public aid or support for religion.[18]

Still the issue is a very present one. The Elementary and Secondary Education Act of 1965 stipulates under Title I that services rendered disadvantaged children under the act must be made available alike to pupils in non-public and public schools. Under Title II books, instructional aids, and library materials are to be supplied non-public school pupils as well as public school pupils although title to all property remains in the hands of a public agency. Under Title III supplementary services initiated under the act are to be made available to non-public as well as to public schools.

This is a very difficult issue with which to deal and one fraught with emotion, but it is an issue that in all candor must be acknowledged.

Problems in the Administration of State Support Programs

Many of the problems associated with the administration of state aid have already been pointed out or inferred. This chapter closes with a brief enumeration by way of summary.

1. Too many states have defined a foundation program and then have failed to fund the program in full. When the dollar amount representing a carefully determined foundation program is arbitrarily reduced, the result is no better than starting with an arbitrary figure in the first place. The question is whether a state program will represent at least a minimum level of educational opportunity or whether the starting point is a dollar figure based on other than educational considerations.
2. There still remain many special purpose grants in a large number of states—grants which often require matching funds from local districts and which are usually more easily matched by wealthy than by poorer districts.

---

[17] *Everson v. Board of Education,* 330 U.S. 1 (1947), p. 15.
[18] *School District of Abington Township, Pennsylvania v. Schempp, Murray v. Curlett,* 83 S. Ct. 1560 (1963). The quotation originally appeared in *Everson v. Board of Education, ibid.,* pp. 31–32.

ISSUES AND PROBLEMS

3. Few states have incentive funds to encourage local school districts to use their tax leeway to undertake experimental projects or to strive for high quality.
4. The use of property tax valuation as a measure of fiscal capacity of local school districts presumes a more accurate appraisal of the worth of property than exists in many school districts. A major step not only in the financing of schools but in the financing of other local government enterprises would be taken if property could be assessed more equitably.
5. The problem remains of avoiding control of local school programs and policies through the state aid act while still being assured that state assistance does not flow to inefficient school districts and submarginal programs.
6. Many states are basing state aid on membership or attendance counts for the previous year. Some provision needs to be made for adjusting the state aid as current year statistics become available.
7. Efforts are being made to provide educational opportunities in the summer time. While few systems have been able to inaugurate year-round programs that require the attendance of part or all of the student body in the summer session, both voluntary enrichment and acceleration programs are becoming increasingly popular. Some school systems have charged tuition for summer programs, but there is a real question as to whether tuition charges in the summer are any more legal than tuition charges during the year. Should state assistance be given summer programs on a basis similar to state assistance for the nine months of the school year?
8. What is the best means of incorporating federal assistance into state aid programs? While federal aid is a very small slice of the total revenue received for schools, it is mounting percentagewise.
9. How can provision be made for periodic review of the elements included in the foundation program and the proportionate share of school costs to be borne by the state and the local school districts? Once legislation is enacted, there is a tendency to perpetuate the status quo. Should the state aid statute provide for periodic review?

CHAPTER V

Local Revenues in the Financing of Public Schools

- From what local sources do school districts receive funds?
- How are property values determined, and how is the property tax administered?
- What non-property taxes are being collected locally?
- How is school district organization related to local tax resources?

Sources of Local Revenue for Schools

The largest single source of revenue collected locally by school districts is the property tax. In most school districts, more than four-fifths of revenues collected locally come from this source; indeed, for the large majority of school districts this is the only local tax source available. In a minority of states legislatures have empowered local taxing authorities to levy certain non-property taxes such as a local income tax, a local sales tax, or a tax on the rental of hotel rooms or on restaurant meals. The levying of these taxes is a matter of local option inaugurated after the endorsing vote of the majority of the electors. In only one state, Pennsylvania, are such non-property taxes widely used by school districts in the support of public education.

The power to levy taxes is not inherent in the school district or in any local governmental unit. This power is granted expressly by the state legislature to the school districts which it has created, and the power must be exercised precisely in the form stipulated by the legislature. School districts may not tap new tax sources without the express authorization of the legislature.

In addition to tax revenues collected locally, a number of school districts receive tuition income for non-resident students attending school within the district. Often this tuition is paid by school districts not offering a complete educational program—for example, by school districts maintaining only an elementary school program and sending their high school pupils to the schools of an adjoining district.

There may be charges for certain services provided by the schools. These charges constitute income although the expenditures associated with the services may exceed the income received in some instances. Examples of charge-financed services are school lunch programs, book sales, and auditorium rentals.

Occasionally gifts and bequests may be made to the board of education. Often these gifts have strings attached and are for specified purposes. The parent-teachers association may be a source of such gifts; a service club may provide a sum in support of some aspect of the school's program; an alumni group may provide funds for the band or for the athletic program. These and other contributions are a minor source of school support but are recognized as income items.

The one overriding fact about local school revenue is that the school district is dependent primarily on the property tax for local school support. Even in the total state-local partnership the local property tax provides on the average more than half of the revenue supporting public education. The percentages of support vary greatly from state to state, with Iowa, New Hampshire, and Nebraska providing more than 80 per cent of the total state-local revenue from the local property tax while Delaware secures less than 20 per cent from this source. Moreover, the differences between districts within a state are marked. When the total valuation of property within a school district is divided by the number of pupils within that district, a very rough measure of local ability to support education is obtained. It is not unusual to find some districts with thirty times the capacity of other districts to support education from local sources.

A second significant fact about the property tax in relation to school support is that this tax is shared with other local governmental units. About four-tenths of the local tax revenue derived from the property tax is allocated to cities, slightly more than three-tenths to school districts, two-tenths to counties, and the remaining tenth to townships and special districts, including metropolitan authorities organized to provide water, sewage disposal, and recreation facilities. This sharing frequently leads to intense competition for the tax dollar. Often the school district by itself is not in a position to decree the extent to which the property base may be utilized to provide school district revenue.

Determination of Property Subject to Taxation

The initial concept of the general property tax was that it would be a tax on the total wealth of individuals and of corporations, but total wealth is not easy to identify or to measure. Down through the years, steps have been taken to make more explicit the exact nature of the property to be taxed. Here, as in other aspects of taxation, different states use different definitions of the property subject to taxation.

In general, property placed on tax rolls falls into three categories: real property, tangible personal property, and intangible personal property.

Real property is defined as land and buildings and other improvement on the land. It is property which is fixed in its location. In the country as a whole, more than 80 per cent of the value of property on tax rolls is real property. Burkhead reports that "residences make up about 54 per cent of the value of locally assessed real estate, and single family dwellings comprise about 90 per cent of residences."[1] Industrial and commercial property and farm property make up most of the remainder of real property valuation.

Tangible personal property is property which has an inherent value of its own and which can be moved should the owner change his residence—for example, household furniture, appliances, automobiles, and jewelry. Machinery and products on inventory are commercial and industrial property often subject to taxation.

Intangible personal property is wealth encompassed in stocks, bonds, insurance policies, mortgages, and kindred investments for which a "paper evidence" of wealth exists.

Every state includes real property on the tax rolls. It cannot be hidden, and its ownership is a matter of public record. Still, there are some exemptions which exclude perhaps as much as 25 per cent of the real property value from the tax rolls. The property of fed-

---

[1] Jesse Burkhead, *State and Local Taxes for Public Education*. Syracuse: Syracuse University Press, 1963, p. 35.

eral, state, and local governments is exempt. Property owned by non-profit educational, religious, or charitable organizations is generally exempt although it may be taxed if it is not used for educational, religious, or charitable purposes. Tax concessions are sometimes made in an effort to attract new industry; thus in Arkansas "capital invested in textile mills is exempt for seven years from the date of the location of such mill."[2] Other exemptions are accomplished by an allowance up to some specified amount for certain classes of property holders such as war veterans. Homestead exemptions fall in this category.

There is a decided trend to remove intangible personal property from the property tax roll. This property is not readily identified and is often inaccurately listed by the holders of intangibles. The income from these investments is taxed by the income tax. Both equity and practicality seem to demand that intangible personal property be removed from local property taxation.

There are many authorities who would likewise espouse removal of tangible personal property from the property tax rolls. Most of the articles taxed are subject to a sales tax at the time of their purchase. Automobiles have been removed as a separate category in most states and are taxed by a license fee. Clothing and other personal effects have usually been exempt. So, in addition to the problems of identification, listing, and appraisal, there is added the accusation of double taxation. New York, Pennsylvania, and Delaware have removed all personal property from the tax base.

As a general conclusion, then, the property tax is based heavily on real property. In an effort to eliminate some of the inequities in the general property tax, exemptions and deductions have caused a diminishment of the tax base. Barr points out:

> Therefore, while the services that are demanded of local government increase both in number and in cost, the principal base available for local taxation has become subject to curtailment.[3]

---

[2] Committee on Tax Education and School Finance, *Action in State Equalization: Case Studies.* Washington: National Education Association of the United States, 1959, p. 19.

[3] W. Monfort Barr, *American Public School Finance.* New York: American Book Co., 1960, p. 116.

Assessment of the Value of Property for Tax Purposes

There are more than sixty million plots of taxable real estate on local tax rolls. To each of these must be attached a value for tax purposes. The starting point is usually the free market value of a piece of property—the price the property is likely to bring on the open market between a willing buyer and a willing seller not acting under duress. This is only the starting point, however, because most tax assessors place a final value on property for tax purposes (the assessed value) at a fraction of the true value. In many states, this fraction is set by constitutional or statutory provisions at a certain percentage of true market value. Even in those states which presumably require assessment at a 100 per cent level, the assessed values set are likely to be below this standard. The Committee on Tax Education and School Finance of the National Education Association concludes:

> In the administration of the property tax no state has achieved a 100 percent level for all local assessment units or for all classes of real property.[4]
> As values in real property have risen and assessments have lagged, the ratio of assessments to cash value has decreased to an absurd level in some states and counties.[5]

The market value of some parcels of property can be determined by the actual sale prices when property changes hands. For these parcels, a ratio can be established between assessed valuation and the selling price. This ratio is usually portrayed as the percentage that assessed valuation is of the selling price. Based on studies of property samples that have been involved in sales, fairly accurate judgments can be made of the extent to which assessments have been debased. For the country as a whole in 1961, the assessed values were reported as less than a third (29 per cent) of fair market value.[6] There is tremendous variation between states. In three

---

[4] Committee on Tax Education and School Finance, National Education Association, *Equalization of Property Assessments*. Washington: National Education Association, 1958, p. 18.

[5] *Ibid.*, p. 20.

[6] U.S. Department of Commerce, Bureau of the Census, *Taxable Property Values*. Census of Governments: 1962, Vol. II. Washington, D.C.: Government Printing Office, 1963, p. 94.

LOCAL REVENUES 63

states—South Carolina, Montana, and Minnesota—assessed values are less than 10 per cent of market value. At the other end of the range, Rhode Island, Delaware, and Connecticut assessed property at more than 50 per cent of its true value. Rhode Island had the highest percentage (67.6%).[7] Likewise, there is tremendous variation between assessing districts within the same state and often within the same tax district. The Ohio Legislative Service Commission reported that in one city in Ohio the assessed valuations of individual properties within the same city varied from 12 per cent to 108 per cent of actual sales values.[8]

The accurate assessment of real property is a complex procedure and requires highly qualified assessors familiar with various types of property ranging from farm land to industrial plants. The majority of assessing officials are still elective officers, usually township or county officials. They lack the professional training needed to cope with the complicated task of valid assessment. According to the Executive Director of the Tax Institute:

> Not only do a large proportion of the assessors lack the technical ability to make accurate assessments, but some of them also practice a deliberate policy of discriminatory assessment. Some favor small homeowners. Others favor industrial enterprises. Under-the-table concessions are offered as an inducement to new enterprises and perhaps also to established enterprises. Local businesses are favored at the expense of concerns whose home office is in another city or state.[9]

Major reforms frequently advocated in property tax assessment include the following:

1. A sufficiently large administrative tax unit so that full-time trained assessors can be appointed and modern data processing equipment used in various aspects of property tax administration, including assessment.
2. State standards which prescribe qualifications and procedures for the selection and retention of trained assessors; a civil service status for all qualified local assessors, with political influence removed. Salaries for assessors at a professional level.

---

[7] *Ibid.*, p. 94.

[8] Ohio Legislative Service Commission, *Local Government Financing Problems in Ohio,* Staff Research Report No. 33. Columbus: Ohio Legislative Service Commission, 1959, p. 23.

[9] Mabel Walker, "Closing Loopholes in State and Local Taxes," an address reported in *Financing the Changing School Program.* Washington: National Education Association, 1962, p. 107.

3. Complete and accurate records listing all property and locations. Accurate up-to-date tax maps. The recording of all sales of property and of sale prices. An examination of sales prices to determine how representative they are and how closely they correspond to assessed valuations.
4. One hundred per cent assessment kept current, rather than a debased assessment.
5. Only one variable in the determination of the level of assessment: the value of property. An end to exemptions and deductions given to special interest groups that constrict the tax base.
6. State-developed tax manuals for assessors, setting forth the factors to be considered in assessing the value of various types of properties.
7. Workshops for assessors to provide in-service upgrading and acquaintance with new developments in property tax administration.
8. Consultant help from the state tax authority to local assessors in placing a proper valuation on unusual and specialized types of property.
9. An assessment of railroad and utility property by state employed tax experts on a state-wide basis with certification of valuations to local tax authorities. (Or the removal of this property from the local tax base to be taxed consistently as a state property tax.)
10. Continuous revision of the tax roll whenever property values change. Periodic scrutiny of the entire tax roll to assure adjustments in valuation that reflect the changes in property values that are constantly occurring.
11. Provisions which require the owners to disclose personal property subject to taxation together with the value of such personal property when it is included in the tax base.
12. Provision for easy access by an aggrieved taxpayer to a board of review where the valuation placed on his property may be appealed, reexamined, and either confirmed or modified. An ultimate recourse available to the taxpayer through action in state courts.
13. State supervision of local assessment by experts employed by the the state to insure accuracy in local tax assessment. Comparison of valuations placed on property by local assessors with selected sampling valuations made by members of the state staff or comparisons of local valuations with the sales prices of property changing ownership. Authority of the state to require adjustments in local valuations.

Built-in factors in present practice make it difficult to bring about many of these reforms. As long as local assessors are elected officials and perform their responsibilities with an eye to re-election, it is difficult to lift valuations to a realistic level. Increasing valuations is not politically popular. Indeed, the whole present pattern of underassessment tends to breed indifference and apathy among taxpayers.

> A homeowner who has just purchased a residence at $15,000 and who is confronted with an assessment of $5,000 is likely to feel that he has been gently treated. If he took the trouble to inspect the assessment rolls, he might find that other similar property was assessed at $4,000. Underassessment is a continued invitation to the perpetuation of ignorance concerning the existence of inequity.[10]

Change is further resisted by those who have been granted exemptions. Not only do these recipients of a favored status wish to maintain the exemptions, but they are opposed to increases in valuation since these increases tend to depreciate the proportionate value of the exemptions or deductions they have gained. For example, the owner of a home with a market value of $15,000 might find his house and lot on the tax roll with an assessed valuation of $3,000. If he lives in a state with a homestead exemption set by statute at $1,000, he pays his tax on a tax base of $2,000. His homestead exemption saves him a third in taxes. Should his assessed valuation be raised to $5,000 with the exemption remaining at $1,000, his taxes would be doubled, his exemption now saving him only one-fifth in taxes. Should the property be assessed at its true value, $15,000, his exemption would save him but one-fifteenth of what he would otherwise pay. When to home owners' exemptions some states add exemptions for war veterans, persons over sixty-five, blind persons, and others in special categories, the remaining taxpayers carry a disproportionate share of taxes. Walker points out:

> This process of granting exemptions feeds upon itself. As more and more exemptions are granted, the tax burden becomes higher upon the persons left to carry the load, so a clamor begins to be heard for even more exemptions.[11]

Still there are forces working in favor of assessment reform. There is now greater public awareness of the tax inequities that do exist. The pressures being placed on the property tax for increased revenue force consideration of broadening the base as well as in-

---
[10] Burkhead, *op. cit.*, p. 75.
[11] Walker, *op. cit.*, p. 105.

creasing tax rates. Many states limit the dollar amount for which school districts may bond themselves for building construction to a percentage of the valuation of the district. Unwarranted low valuations restrict bonding capacity and prevent the erection of needed school buildings. Unreasonable ceilings thus create pressures for reform.

State aid to local school districts is increasing in many states. Equalization aid is paid in varying amounts to school districts after the district's local contribution to the joint state-local program has been determined. The local contribution is usually based on a millage rate applied to the property valuation of the school district. This has led in some instances to competitive under-assessment by local districts in order to appear poor and to garner a greater measure of state funds. Many legislators now resist increases in state aid until the basis of local effort is more equitably determined. Sometimes an effort is made to resolve this problem by the use of a figure called an equalized valuation. A reviewing tax authority at the county or state level (or both) makes studies of the proportion that assessed valuation is of true valuation in the various school districts. The total assessed valuation for each district is then adjusted upward or downward until there is parity for all districts at the same fraction of fair market value. This new figure is the base against which millage rates are applied in computing the local contribution in a joint state-local formula for school support. In most states this figure is a "paper figure" and is used only when the amount of state assistance to local units of government is being determined. Why local taxing districts should not be required to adjust valuations so that the total of assessed valuations conforms to the equalized valuation is difficult to explain. In the years ahead, such conformity will be increasingly required. The pressure for additional state aid may be a major factor bringing about local tax reform. The Committee on Tax Education and School Finance of the National Education Association suggests:

> The distribution of state funds to equalize educational opportunities, if based on assessed values, may facilitate the inauguration of a state assessment equalization program if timed to coincide with the inauguration of a new or improved school foundation program.[12]

---

[12] Committee on Tax Education and School Finance, *Action in State Equalization: Case Studies, op. cit.,* p. 44.

Establishment of a Tax Rate

The property valuation of a school district constitutes the local bank against which a draft is drawn annually for the current operation of a school system. The amount of the draft is determined by the budget adopted by the board of education and the draft is issued typically in the form of a millage rate. A rate of 1 mill is the same as a rate of $1 per $1,000 of assessed valuation.

In its simplest form, the determination of the tax rate for school purposes and of a property holder's tax would follow the steps illustrated below:

Determination of the tax rate:

Steps	Example
1. Adoption of the budget of the school district for the ensuing year.	Budget of $2,880,000 adopted.
2. Listing of the assessed valuations of individual parcels of property on the tax roll and determination of the total assessed valuation of the school district.	The total assessed valuation of the school district: $240,000,000.
3. Division of the budget adopted by the assessed valuation of the district to determine the tax rate for school purposes.	$2,880,000 ÷ $240,000,000 = .012, a rate of $12 per $1,000 of assessed valuation or 12 mills.

Computation of an individual property owner's tax:

Steps	Example
1. Determination of the assessed valuation of the individual property owner's property as listed on the tax roll.	Valuation of house and lot of property holder assessed at $6,000.
2. Multiplication of the assessed valuation by the tax rate to determine the dollar amount of the tax for school purposes.	$6,000 × .012 = $72, the amount of school taxes to be paid by the property holder.

The example has been given in its simplest form. There are many ramifications in different states which complicate the procedure outlined.

In a number of states, the board of education is not entirely free to act upon the school budget. Public budget hearings may be required by statute before final action may be taken by the board. Indeed public hearings are a sound procedure for the board to follow, whether they are required or not. In some districts, particularly small districts in rural areas, states may require that the favorable vote of the electors be secured prior to certification of the school district's budget. The task of the board under these circumstances is to recommend a budget to the electors.

Some districts are what is known as fiscally dependent school districts. Before the budgets in these school districts may be adopted, they must be submitted to and approved by the legislative or executive authority of some other governmental unit. By state statute, all districts or certain classified districts in a state may be decreed fiscally dependent districts. Some districts are "special act" school districts in that they were brought into being by a special act of the legislature and possess characteristics and governing procedures which differ from those districts created under the general acts of the legislature. A number of these special act school districts in large cities are fiscally dependent school districts, and the board of education must submit its budget to the mayor or to the city council for approval before the budget may be promulgated. In fiscally dependent districts, then, the budget of a school district is subject to review and approval by an independent agency outside of the school district such as the chief executive or the finance officer of a municipal or county government or the governing council of the municipality or county in which the school district is located. Sometimes special local finance committees, either appointed or elected, are authorized by state legislatures to review the budgets of all governmental agencies operating at the local level, including school districts, and to make the final determination of budget amounts and tax rates.

Those who advocate fiscally dependent school districts do so on the grounds that different local governmental units share the tax base. Not only is the school district dependent on the property tax for local revenue but so are townships, cities, counties, and any special districts which may have been established. It is maintained that unless there is compulsory coordination of the budgets of these governing units, the total budget requests are likely to be beyond the reasonable tax capacity of the geographic area served by these overlapping bodies. Some review agency is needed to determine the priorities represented in the various budget proposals.

The majority of school districts are fiscally independent. Their budget, once set by vote of the board or by vote of the electors in the district, is translated into a millage levy, added without change to the millage levies of other local governmental units, and levied and collected by the governmental officer empowered with the responsibility for tax collection, frequently the county treasurer. Revenues received on the school's tax levy are paid directly to the school district treasury.

Those who advocate the fiscal independence of school districts point out that school districts are creatures of the state, not subdivisions of municipal governments. It makes as much sense, they claim, to have a city council review the budget of the school board as it would to have the board of education review the budget proposed by the city council. These are coordinate bodies. The responsibilities of each are so large that legislatures have generally decreed that school districts and local governmental units should have separate governing boards. A board of education works on budget matters and on the financial affairs of the district throughout the year and spends days on the budget presented to it by its professional administrators. This wealth of information is not available to a review board and cannot possibly be gained in the evening or two generally allotted school budget hearings. Most review boards, even those organized as separate finance committees not otherwise connected with any governmental unit, are weighted in their composition so that schools are represented neither in proportion to the tax dollars levied by schools nor in proportion to the cruciality of education as an essential governmental function. It is contended that fiscally dependent school districts generally come off second best whenever there is a head-on conflict between school district needs and the needs of municipal governments. Coordination is necessary, but it must be achieved in the give and take of voluntary compromise, not by the subordination of the school district to another governmental authority.

Still another factor which affects the preparation of school budgets and the determination of the tax levy is the constitutional or statutory ceiling on millage levies which is found in more than three-fourths of the states. These ceilings are usually expressed as maximum tax rates which can be levied. Sometimes the ceilings are maximum rates for school district levies, sometimes maximum rates on the property tax which can be levied by all governmental units in any given tax district. Occasionally provision is made for the maximum rate to be exceeded if the extra levy is approved by a specified majority of the electors.

Many of these millage ceilings were written into statutes in the depression years. Some of the constitutional provisions were invoked before the turn of the century. Most of the ceilings are unrealistic in terms of the needs which must now be served by the property tax and in terms of the revenue which the property tax can reasonably be expected to yield. Two steps can be taken: millage limits and debt limitations can be raised or removed; property reassessment can broaden the base of property taxed so that present millage levies are more productive in the revenues they yield.

Collection of Property Taxes

The board of education certifies its tax levy to the tax collecting agency for the geographic area in which the school district is located. Any individual property owner's tax is an aggregate of the various rates levied by local governmental entities. The tax notice sent the property holder generally delineates the tax rates levied by each governing body, and graphic diagrams and charts are sometimes employed to acquaint him with the distribution being made of his tax dollar.

The major reform being advocated in connection with the collection of property taxes is provision for paying the tax in monthly or quarterly installments. In many states, property taxes are still payable on an annual basis. Modern data processing methods make installment recording manageable, and any extra cost would be more than offset by fewer delinquencies. The typical taxpayer does not set aside funds from each month's pay check to prepare for the impact of an annual tax bill. A tax of $480, for example, payable in one fell swoop disrupts the bank accounts of most families, whereas a monthly payment of $40 is more easily absorbed.

Another measure being taken is to place tax collecting officials, such as the county treasurer, on a specified salary rather than employing a fee basis for collection. Prompt identification of delinquent taxes is being stressed with more assiduous pursuit of past due accounts.

Non-Property Taxes for Public Schools

When state funds and local property taxes do not yield the revenues needed for the educational program the people of a school district wish to provide, and when there is widespread resistance to increases in the property tax rate, efforts are made to find other sources of taxation at the local level. Only the limits in the ingenuity of the mind of man have confined the wide-ranging proposals for taxing almost every conceivable product and every imaginable activity. Of course, the authority of local governments to tax must be granted by the state.

The first local non-property taxes were levied by cities rather than by school districts. New York City led with a tax on retail sales in 1934. Philadelphia followed with a sales tax but substituted a flat rate income tax in 1939. The most sweeping provision for local non-property taxes was inaugurated by the State of Pennsylvania in 1947 when the legislature voted to permit local units of government, including school districts, to levy any tax not levied by the state. More than 2,000 school districts in Pennsylvania have levied some form of local non-property tax.[13]

Among the local non-property taxes which have been levied in one or more of the fifty states are the following:

> A tax on general retail sales or on gross receipts.
> A selective sales tax on specific consumer items such as tobacco, alcoholic beverages, or motor fuel.
> A local income or payroll tax.
> A tax on restaurant meals paid by the consumer.
> A tax on the occupancy of hotel rooms.
> An admissions or entertainment tax paid by the consumer as a percentage of the ticket price.
> Utility taxation: a percentage of the monthly utility bill or a flat fee for a utility installation such as a meter fee or a fee for a telephone outlet.
> A tax on each vending machine in operation.
> A license to operate a specified business or to practice certain pro-

---

[13] Barr, *op. cit.*, p. 101.

fessions. Examples are license fees which must be paid in order to operate a liquor store, a restaurant, a theater, a hotel, a trailer park, a car dealership.
A local license fee to operate a motor vehicle.
A tax on deed transfers when property changes ownership.
A per capita or head tax.
A local poll tax.

This is by no means an exhaustive list, but it does include those taxes which have produced substantial revenue. The retail sales tax has been the most productive of these taxes, with taxes on income ranking second.

Burkhead has summarized the status of local non-property taxes levied by local units of government:

> Although the aggregate of local nonproperty tax revenue stabilized at about 12 or 13 per cent of local tax collections in the decade of the 1950's, this development has been significantly important in some states. In 17 states in 1960, local nonproperty taxes were less than 5 per cent of total local taxes, but in New York State they were 23 per cent of the total; in Pennsylvania, 25.9 per cent; and in Alabama (local sales taxes) they were 43.7 per cent. Moreover, these levies are important for cities with population of more than 1,000,000. With the recent addition of Detroit, all of the nation's five largest cities now have local nonproperty levies.[14]

In general, cities have been authorized to use local non-property taxes more frequently than have school districts. This does not preclude some indirect assistance to school districts, however, as some leeway may be produced by the municipalities receiving revenue from non-property taxes which would otherwise have to come from the property tax. Presumably a greater portion of property tax income may then go to the school district.

A major factor which deters school districts from entering the non-property tax field is lack of the basic records needed to effectively administer many of the non-property taxes. Income tax returns made available to either the state or federal governments do not designate the school district of which the taxpayer is a resident; utility bills are not associated with the school district of residence. Local collection of non-property taxes is an inefficient and costly operation. If school districts are to utilize non-property taxes, they should band together into regional units or else do the collection

---

[14] Burkhead, *op. cit.*, pp. 99–100.

on the state level with the revenue being fed back to the individual districts on a per pupil or some other unit basis.

Of course, the duplication of taxes already being levied is an important argument against local non-property taxes. Those taxes producing greatest revenue have usually been preempted by either the federal or state levels of government. In many states, taxpayers already pay federal and state income taxes. To add a payroll tax brings cries of anguish that double taxation has now been stretched to triple taxation. The annoyance of a multiplicity of taxes scores heavily against non-property taxes; the appellation of "nuisance taxes" is often deserved.

The lack of uniformity between school districts in levying non-property taxes may not only cause confusion but may result in the movement of business from one area to another in order to avoid taxation. There are allegations, although no clear-cut evidence, that sales taxes levied in cities have contributed to the move to suburban shopping centers.

Many of the non-property taxes are regressive in their effect and place a greater proportionate burden in terms of ability to pay on those with low incomes.

On the positive side, the proponents of local non-property taxes point out that these taxes do bring additional tax revenues not otherwise available to school districts and that these revenues either buttress the property tax or, where rates are unduly high, bring tax relief. Most of the non-property taxes respond more quickly than property taxes to changes in the economic welfare of the country; they bring responsiveness and flexibility to the local tax picture.

School District Organization in Relation to Local Revenues

The fundamental purpose of school district organization is to achieve a better educational program for children and young people. There are many criteria of a good school district, but two absolute requisites are enough students to make a diversified secondary school program possible at reasonable cost and sufficient funds procurable from local sources which, together with state aid, will provide adequate financial support for both operating expense and capital outlay. There are thousands of districts in the United States, indeed the majority of districts, which cannot meet these two requisites. All over the country district annexations and reorganizations are taking place, usually by voluntary means, sometimes by state mandate.

The major consequences of carefully planned school district organizations are the following:

1. A larger tax base for both operating and capital outlay expenses. The larger base may make possible the issuance of bonds to provide new school buildings. Small school districts are frequently deterred from issuing bonds by the inadequacy of their tax base.
2. The larger tax base is more stable and less subject to fluctuation in assessed value. The administration of the reorganized district as a single taxing unit tends to bring about more uniform assessment practices.
3. The disparity in the fiscal ability of different school districts to support education is reduced. Armstrong and Farner have estimated that "a complete reorganization of California elementary school districts could reduce variations in wealth per child from the present extremes of 7000:1 to 22:1."[15]
4. The local tax equalization which results as school districts are enlarged reduces the amount of state aid needed for inter-district equalization. This freeing of state funds may create tax leeway at the state level to increase the foundation amount.
5. In reorganized districts, all citizens have a voice in the total school program and in tax and fiscal matters. When high school pupils are sent out of an elementary district as tuition pupils, the voters in the district of residence have no direct voice in the governance of the high school their young people attend.
6. A more highly qualified central administrative staff is available in the reorganized district. Educational and financial affairs are managed by more competent personnel. Consultant services from the central staff can be made available to all schools in the reorganized district.
7. In some instances the reorganized district is large enough to make the levying of local non-property taxes feasible.
8. Reorganized districts generally provide a better educational program with more efficiency for the tax dollar expended, but not necessarily at lower net cost or at a lower tax rate. Reorganizations often make possible badly needed new school buildings which could not otherwise be erected, but to build them the

---

[15] Herbert C. Armstrong and Frank Farner, "Financial Support for Public Education," John A. Vieg et al., *California Local Finance*. Stanford: Stanford University Press, 1960, p. 288. Quoted in Burkhead, *op. cit.*, p. 45.

tax rate must go up. Reorganizations should generally be advocated not on the basis of tax savings but because of better education and a more effective use of the tax dollar.

In some states, particularly southern states, districts are organized along county lines, and reorganization is not a pressing need. In other states, even when substantial district reorganization has taken place, districts are banding together to establish a superimposed intermediate unit to provide specialized services which separate districts cannot provide economically by themselves. Examples of such services are special classes for the physically and mentally handicapped and the emotionally disturbed, the services of a centrally established child guidance clinic, a regional library and materials center, health services including vision and hearing testing, the administration of aptitude and achievement testing programs, and the specialized consultant services of central staff members in the different curriculum areas. Sometimes intermediate units become the legal school district, supporting and operating a regional community college.

Intermediate districts may receive support from state funds, from appropriations made by the individual school districts which comprise it on a per pupil or other unit basis, or by a direct tax upon local residents or local property. Such a levy must be authorized by the legislature and is generally a property tax at a low millage rate. This tax is added onto the levy for school purposes in the constituent districts comprising the intermediate unit; frequently it must be voted into effect by a majority of electors residing in the intermediate unit. In the United States as a whole, the revenue receipts of intermediate districts approximate 2 per cent of total school revenue.

The Property Tax: Maligned but Munificent

The first flush of experimentation and excitement over non-property taxation has given way to a more sober appraisal. The problems of tax duplication, costly administration, and the nuisance factor have combined to slow widespread adoption. Less than 15 per cent of local non-property taxes are collected by school districts. There is a growing feeling that non-property taxes for schools tend to be used as a palliative for temporary relief when the more fundamental problem may be the need for revitalizing the property tax base or strengthening the state aid program. Burkhead points out that the levying of local non-property taxes "may simply reflect an abnegation of state political and fiscal responsibility."[16]

The property tax is the target of much criticism. It is no longer an accurate measure of the total wealth of an individual. Its base is riddled by exemptions and deductions. It is a regressive tax, particularly for retired persons or others on fixed low incomes. It is poorly administered, particularly in respect to assessment practices. The increases in the property tax rates in some tax jurisdictions have outdistanced increases in the incomes of the property owners who must pay the tax.

Yet there is much to be said for the property tax. It complements the pattern of taxation at state and federal levels and its regressivity is reduced when viewed in the context of a total tax package, especially if the property base can be restored and efficient assessment practices can be established. Of great importance is the role of the property tax as the one vehicle which permits the local resident to translate his desires for education directly into action by providing the wherewithal for a school program he wishes to support or by drawing the purse strings tight when there is disapproval. Benson states, "In spite of its patent disadvantages, the case for the property tax is essentially the case for local government."[17]

Most of all, the property tax yields a substantial amount in terms of dollars raised. It produces. If the property tax had not responded with increased revenues in the last ten years, schools today would be even more crowded, teachers less well paid. Yet with the increase in dollar revenue, the burden of the tax "measured in national income terms" is about one-third less in the 1960s than in the 1920s.[18] A lower proportion of the national income is siphoned off in property taxes than was the case forty years ago. The potential of the property tax is not yet exhausted. In most states, at least one-half of the financial support of the schools will continue to come from the property tax. It is maligned but munificent.

---

[16] Burkhead, *op. cit.*, p. 100.
[17] Charles S. Benson, *The Economics of Public Education.* Boston: Houghton Mifflin Co., 1961, p. 171.
[18] Burkhead, *op. cit.*, p. 26.

CHAPTER VI

State Taxation for Public Schools

- What are the sources of state revenue for schools?
- How are state funds allocated to education?
- What differences exist between states in their taxing capacity and in their state support of schools?
- What trends are occurring in state school finance?

Even when property tax assessments are equalized at the local level, the resultant tax base is not nearly large enough in most districts to provide the revenue needed for the schools. State tax support is required, and in the country as a whole 39 per cent of all costs of public schools are paid from state sources. It is apparent that educators must be concerned with the nature of state revenues. The adequacy of school support depends as much on the productivity of state taxes as upon the carefully worked out state aid formulas which have been of so much concern.

Sources of State Revenues

More than 85 per cent of local tax revenues are derived from the property tax. More than 80 per cent of federal revenues come from individual and corporate income taxes. State revenues are diffused over the tax spectrum and draw on many sources. The taxes most frequently levied and the amounts of yield for 1964 are set forth in Table 8.

The general sales tax or tax on gross receipts brings in about one-fourth of state tax revenues. In all but seven of the states levying this tax, this tax measure secures more revenue than any other state tax source. The range in the tax rate on sales is from two per cent to five per cent, but the modal rate is three per cent (in 18 of the states). Some states exempt purchases of food and medicine from the tax, thereby reducing the regressiveness of the tax.

The general sales tax is an excellent producer of revenue which

TABLE 8

State Tax Collections in 1964[1]

Type of tax	Number of states levying taxes of this type	Amount of tax yield (in millions)	Per cent of total yield
General sales or gross receipts	37	$ 6,134	25.3
Selective sales	50	7,870	32.5
Individual net income	36	3,363	13.9
Corporation income	37	1,699	7.0
License fees	50	3,060	12.6
Property	45	727	3.0
Death and gift	49	658	2.7
Severance	29	489	2.0
Other	#	244	1.0
		$24,244	100.0

responds quickly to changes in the economy. Burkhead predicts that the general sales tax with exemptions for food and drugs "is the levy which is likely to win acceptance in the remaining non-sales tax states over the next several years."[2]

A selective sales tax is a tax levied on a particular item of purchase with its own tax attached thereto. All states tax motor fuels and alcoholic beverages, and all but three states tax the sales of tobacco products. Taxes on the services purchased from utility companies and on amounts of insurance underwritten are generally classed as selective sales taxes, as are taxes on pari-mutuel betting.

Sometimes other items in the service category are taxed—for example, the amounts paid barbers and beauticians. Or hotel and motel accommodations may be taxed a percentage of the bill paid. When a fixed percentage is extended to cover a wide variety of services, this tax should probably be grouped with the general sales tax rather than the selective sales tax.

On the theoretical grounds of its relation to ability to pay, the net income tax is generally regarded as the most equitable tax that

---

[1] Source: Preliminary figures for 1964 derived from N.E.A. Committee on Educational Finance, "State Taxes in 1964," *C.E.F. Report,* Number 11. Washington: The Committee, March, 1965, p. 16.

Other taxes are too disparate to classify and to assign frequencies for the number of states making levies.

[2] Jesse Burkhead, *State and Local Taxes for Public Education.* Syracuse: Syracuse University Press, 1963, p. 93.

STATE TAXATION FOR PUBLIC SCHOOLS

can be levied. Its major drawback as a state revenue producer is that this levy represents a tax duplication, for it is the major means used in financing the federal government. Of course, the rates at the state level are much lower and are not as progressive.

Some kind of license fee is charged in all fifty of the states. All but one state, Hawaii, has a state fee for the licensing of motor vehicles and for operators' licenses. These fees relating to automobiles and their operation account for more than fifty per cent of all revenues accruing from license charges. Other types of licenses are corporation business licenses and hunting and fishing licenses.

Before the turn of the century, property taxes levied by the state were the major source of state revenue. The dominant interest of local governments in this tax has caused it to be relinquished in large part at the state level. It currently provides but 3 per cent of state tax revenue. It is still on the books as a state tax in some form in forty-five states, however.

Severance taxes are taxes paid on the removal of natural resources from the land—minerals and timber for example. The severance tax sometimes operates to keep forest crops on the land until maturity. Besides bringing in revenue, it compensates a state somewhat for the removal of natural resources, some of which cannot be replaced.

Most states levy more than one of the taxes enumerated in Table 8. Twenty-three states, for example, have both a general sales tax and an individual net income tax. They are likely, also, to levy other forms of the taxes listed.

One other source of state revenue, which cannot be classed as a tax, is the revenue derived from so-called "permanent funds," which had their origin in grants of land set aside for education.

> In England schools were endowed with land holdings to assure their continued financial well-being. In the English colonies, individuals began granting land after the pattern of the mother country for the purpose of improving education. The New England towns took up the practice and made gifts of land to the schools ranging from forty to sixty acres.[3]

Connecticut established the first state "permanent fund" for edu-

---

[3] Central Michigan School Administrators' Research Association, "New Light on Federal Support," *Research Report,* Vol. I, No. 6. Mt. Pleasant, Michigan: Central Michigan School Administrators' Research Association, December 1960, p. 6.

cation in 1795 and incorporated in the fund monies earlier set aside from the sale of western boundary lands. By 1830 nearly all of the original thirteen states had established endowment funds. The federal grants of land accorded states as they were admitted into the Union made possible the creation of additional "permanent funds." There were other land grants, also, such as those provided under the Internal Improvement Act of 1841. Some direct money grants were made by Congress—the Surplus Revenue "Deposit" Act of 1836, for example.

These educational endowment funds were not always well administered. In some cases the funds were diverted to other government activities. In a number of states the fund remains only as a recorded debt which the legislature honors by annual or biennial appropriations. When the fund has been well managed, interest on invested money or the income from the leases of land provide revenue for school purposes. In the country as a whole, however, less than 2 per cent of all state school revenue accrues from this source.

Allocation of State Funds to Education

The revenue sources outlined may be utilized for the many functions of state government as well as for education, with the exception of the permanent or endowment fund set up for educational purposes and particular taxes which are earmarked for the use of education. In most states, the bulk of state revenues flow into the state general fund and are not earmarked. From this fund, support goes to the schools in the form of legislative appropriations.

States which have relied on earmarked sources have found that income from these sources has not risen commensurately with the increases in school population and in educational costs. A foundation program of the type outlined in Chapter III needs the flexibility provided by general fund appropriations. One reason that states hang on to earmarked funds is that educators are reluctant to renounce any revenue until states assume the full responsibility for seeing that a foundation formula is underwritten. In some instances, certain taxes are earmarked for the schools by constitutional provision, so that a constitutional change is necessary to modify the pattern of revenue. Most earmarked sources are mandated by statute rather than by constitution, however. Portions of

STATE TAXATION FOR PUBLIC SCHOOLS 81

nearly all of the major state revenue sources have been earmarked for schools in at least some states: income taxes, sales taxes, taxes on utilities, poll taxes, and licenses and fees. Louisiana and Texas have earmarked major portions of the severance tax for schools.

In the country as a whole, four-fifths of state school revenues come from legislative appropriations. Slightly under one-fifth of state school income is derived from earmarked taxes. Income from "permanent funds" makes up the last small slice.

In terms of the distribution of funds to local school districts as decreed by present legislative appropriations, statutes, and, in some instances, constitutional provisions, the theory of relatively heavy weighting of funds for general purposes on an equalization basis has not yet been realized in practice.

> Twenty-one states distribute more than 50 per cent of all of their funds as general-purpose flat-grants and six distribute more than 50 per cent as special-purpose flat-grants. In only 18 states are more than 50 per cent of the funds distributed as general-purpose equalizing grants and in only one state, Indiana, are more than 50 per cent distributed as special-purpose equalizing funds.[4]

Differences Between the States in State Support of Schools and in Taxing Capacity

The wide variations in revenue from state sources in comparing one state with another have already been presented.[5] Delaware, for example, derives more than 75 per cent of public school income from state sources. At the other extreme, Nebraska provides less than 10 per cent of income from state taxes. Appropriations actually voted at the state level bear but a slight relationship to tax capability.

One procedure for determining a rough measure of the capacity of a state to levy taxes employs a measure termed "residual personal income." Residual income is computed by deducting from the total income of persons within any given state payments for personal taxes and $800 per person for food, clothing, and shelter. This figure is then divided by the number of school-age children within

---
[4] Roe L. Johns and Edgar L. Morphet, *Financing the Public Schools*. Englewood Cliffs, N.J.: Prentice-Hall, Inc., 1960, p. 241.
[5] *Supra*, p. 31.

each state. A study reported in 1959, using 1955 data, shows that the extremes are represented by $6,778 residual income per child in Connecticut as contrasted with $418 residual personal income per child in Mississippi. "The eight richest states have, on the average, more than five times as many disposable dollars as the eight poorest states."[6] Table 9 shows the residual personal income of these contrasting states and relates these data to the effort made in behalf of education as measured by the percentage of total personal income that goes for school expenditures. This study was made sometime ago; so the amounts shown are considerably less than they would be today. The same marked variations between states are likely to exist, however.

TABLE 9

COMPARISON OF THE EIGHT LOW STATES IN TERMS OF RESIDUAL PERSONAL INCOME WITH THE EIGHT HIGH STATES[7]

States	Residual Personal Income	School Expenditures as Per Cent of Personal Income	Per Pupil Current Expenditure
LOW STATES:			
Mississippi	$ 418	3.4	$ 132
Arkansas	755	3.0	138
South Carolina	865	3.5	161
Alabama	1,079	3.3	166
Kentucky	1,284	2.4	151
North Carolina	1,401	3.2	171
Tennessee	1,443	2.9	170
West Virginia	1,456	3.2	179
HIGH STATES:			
Massachusetts	5,046	2.2	295
Illinois	5,691	2.2	311
California	5,929	2.7	330
New York	5,956	2.5	365
Nevada	5,980	2.6	292
New Jersey	6,183	2.4	338
Delaware	6,305	2.0	322
Connecticut	6,778	2.1	306

Even with the greater effort made by the eight low states, the dollar amount expended per pupil averages only half the per pupil expenditures the eight highest states are able to mount.

---

[6] Educational Policies Commission, *National Policy and the Financing of the Public Schools*. Washington: National Education Association, 1959, pp. 15–16.
[7] *Ibid.*, pp. 16–17.

A factor which is not necessarily related to tax capacity tends to keep the levying of taxes by the various states somewhat in line with each other. With the mobility which exists today between states, corporations and individuals search for states which offer a "favorable tax climate." The fact that a state cannot rise much above its neighbors in its tax load without courting possible loss of industry often serves as a brake on needed tax increases.

Trends in State School Support

By way of summary, the following trends can be discerned in state school support:

1. State tax revenues are increasing. Not only is there a gross increase in dollar amount, but the amount per capita is increasing. Not once in the last decade has this trend of increased income been interrupted, although the trend line tends to advance in two-year spurts because of legislative enactments in states which have biennial sessions.

2. In spite of these increases, the state government is hardly increasing its tax income in proportion to the increases in local property taxes. In some respects, local property taxes have been more responsive to increased governmental needs than have state taxes. This is true for many governmental services as well as for education.

3. More and more states are incorporating both sales and income taxes in their state tax framework.

4. The revenue from sales taxes has increased markedly, and sales taxes now constitute the most important single source of state tax revenue.

5. In an increasing number of states a percentage tax is being placed on payment for services such as hotel and motel bills, barber and beautician charges, and some professional services. In effect, taxes for services as well as for goods purchased are being added to the sales tax base.

6. Three-fifths of the states having income taxes now have a mechanism for withholding state income taxes from payrolls. More than half of these withholding provisions have been adopted in the last ten years.

7. In recent decades the overlapping of federal and state taxes has increased as each level of government sought new tax sources.

The greatest overlapping occurs in the duplication of the income tax; there are, however, some evidences of administrative coordination. The income tax in twelve states is now based on the federal income tax base. More than half of the states have entered agreements with the federal government for the exchange of tax information. Auditing procedures can be coordinated and tax avoidance held to a minimum.

8. There are diminishing returns percentagewise from the state property tax. Currently less than 3 per cent of state revenues come from this source.

9. In terms of the amount of revenue allocated to education, there is increasing reliance on appropriations rather than on earmarked funds. The percentage of state revenues derived from "permanent-fund" income is decreasing.

10. More than ten billion dollars are now derived from state sources for the support of public elementary and secondary schools.

CHAPTER VII

The Role of Federal Government in Financing Education

- How has the federal government given financial assistance to education?
- What are the pros and cons of federal aid to education?
- Should federal aid represent general support or should it be categorical aid?
- What other issues underlie the participation of the federal government in the financing of education?

Federal Measures for Financial Assistance to Education

The delegates to the Constitutional Convention which founded the United States made no express provision for federal activity in education. Under the Tenth Amendment to the Constitution, education, not being a power delegated to the federal government by the Constitution itself, was "reserved to the states respectively, or to the people." Federal activities in the educational field, which have grown through the years, are performed under the expanding interpretations granted the general welfare clause of the Constitution.

Land grants to encourage the support of education. The fact that the founders of the Constitution made no provision for federal educational programs cannot be construed as a lack of national interest in education. There has always been concern that the various states meet the obligation delegated to them for the establishment of programs of education for the youth of each state. This was demonstrated as early as 1785 when the Continental Congress provided that one section of every township should be set aside for the use of public schools.

After the Constitution had been adopted, Congress was given responsibility for policies concerning the regulation and disposition of the national domain. With the advent of Ohio as a state in 1802, provision was made in the enabling act for the sixteenth section of every township to be earmarked for school purposes. Each state admitted to the Union after this date, until Alaska and Hawaii were admitted, had a similar stipulation in the enabling act, except that in some states two sections were set aside in each township, and in a few states four sections were allotted. No land grants for public elementary and secondary school purposes were required in the enabling acts establishing Alaska and Hawaii as states. Pierce summarizes the land grant program:

> Altogether, thirty states received land grants for the support of public schools. The thirteen original colonies and the three states originating from them (Vermont, Maine, and West Virginia), received no land grants for education, nor did Kentucky which was admitted before the policy began, nor Texas which was annexed.[1]

Unfortunately, many states used these lands unwisely, often failing to hold them in trust. Lands were sometimes sold at relatively low prices with an eye to attracting settlers rather than for the purpose of building up a financial endowment for the public schools. Still, these early land grants were some indication of a national concern that schools be established and encouraged.

Federal assistance for programs of vocational education. The land grants can be characterized as general aid to education in that the federal government attached few strings to the use of the funds derived from the land—in contrast to nearly all other federal assistance which has been enacted down through the years. Most federal legislation has been brought into being for the purpose of advancing instruction in certain designated fields.

An excellent example of such "categorical" assistance is the Smith-Hughes Act of 1917, inaugurated to encourage vocational education in the public schools. Until the passage of this act the program of the high schools had been largely academic in character. Although some large cities and some states had established separate vocational or technical schools, school boards as a general rule had been loathe to assume a responsibility for vocational education. Vocational education was expensive and industry was presumed to have the responsibility for the preparation of workers. Retention of all youth through high school with differentiation of programs to

---

[1] Truman M. Pierce, *Federal, State and Local Government in Education.* New York: The Center for Applied Research in Education, Inc., 1964, p. 25.

meet particular educational and vocational needs was then still more in the realm of theory than in practice.

The advent of World War I, however, underlined the shortage of skilled manpower. The United States could no longer depend on immigration as a source of skilled craftsmen and the European apprenticeship system seemed unlikely to become the pattern in the United States. The growing recognition that the war potential depended as much on skilled vocational productivity as on the armed services was a major factor in the establishment of federal subsidies for vocational education. The need for training agricultural workers was also recognized, and the total program encompassed courses in industry, trade, commerce, agriculture, and home economics.

Between 1917 and 1963 the pattern of Smith-Hughes assistance was extended somewhat by a series of acts: the George-Reed Act (1929); the George-Ellzey Act (1934); the George-Dean Act (1936); the George-Barden Act (1946). Among the vocational fields added to those initially stipulated were the distributive occupations, practical nurse training, and the fishery trades.

In 1961 President Kennedy asked the Secretary of Health, Education, and Welfare to appoint a representative committee of experts in the field of vocational education to review existing vocational education laws and to make recommendations for future legislation. In his education message to the Congress on January 29, 1963, President Kennedy called for "new grant-in-aid legislation aimed at meeting the needs of individuals in all age groups for vocational training in occupations where they can find employment in today's diverse labor markets."[2] The result was the Vocational Education Act of 1963, a much broader attack on the problems of vocational education than had been heretofore mounted.

The new act calls for vocational education programs to prepare individuals for gainful employment in the wide spectrum of today's specialized vocations, including business and office occupations. The state administering agency is required to revise the program as manpower needs and job opportunities shift. Programs of professional preparation requiring a baccalaureate degree are excluded

---

[2] John F. Kennedy, "Message from the President Relative to a Proposed Program for Education, January 29, 1963." Charles A. Quattlebaum, *Federal Legislation Concerning Education and Training, Enactments of 1963 and Issues of 1964.* Washington: United States Government Printing Office, 1964, p. 139.

from the act, but vocational guidance and counseling is recognized as an essential function in the vocational education process and may be included in state plans to receive federal assistance.

There have been and are definite federal controls in connection with the administration of vocational education grants. The statewide program of vocational education must be submitted by the state educational authority to the United States Office of Education for approval. Funds, however, are channeled from the federal government to the various state school authorities who administer the program in the respective states.

As outlined by Charles A. Quattlebaum, the state plan for using federal funds in connection with the Vocational Education Act of 1963 may include:

1. Vocational education for persons attending high school;
2. Vocational education for persons who have completed or left high school and who are available for full-time study in preparation for entering the labor market;
3. Vocational education for persons . . . who have already entered the labor market and who need training or retraining to achieve stability or advancement in employment;
4. Vocational education for persons who have academic, socioeconomic, or other handicaps that prevent them from succeeding in the regular vocational education program;
5. Construction of area vocational education school facilities;
6. Ancillary services and activities to assure quality in all vocational education programs, such as teacher training and supervision, program evaluation, and state administration and leadership.[3]

The act provides for a work-study program for young people between the ages of fifteen and twenty-one who must have earnings from part-time employment in order to remain in an approved vocational training program. They are given employment up to fifteen hours a week in the local school system or in some other public agency or institution, with federal funds underwriting the compensation received.

The act also provides for the experimental establishment of some

---

[3] Charles A. Quattlebaum, *Federal Legislation Concerning Education and Training, Enactments of 1963 and Issues of 1964*. Washington: United States Government Printing Office, 1964, p. 22. Under item 3 of this listing, persons who are receiving training allowances under certain other federal grants such as the Manpower Development and Training Act are excluded.

residential vocational education schools, particularly in urban areas having a substantial number of high school drop-outs or a high level of youth unemployment. These schools are designed for young people fifteen to twenty-one years of age who are deemed to need full-time study on a residential basis in order to profit fully from a program of vocational education.

Federal funds to states for vocational education are disbursed according to an objective formula taking into consideration the number of persons in the population between the ages of fifteen and sixty-five and the per capita income of each state. Matching funds are required so that in no case does federal assistance exceed 50 per cent of the cost of carrying out the state plan.

Depression measures and acts linked with combatting unemployment. During the depression of the 1930s many educational measures were passed by Congress. The grants given schools came about not so much because of a concern for improving the school curriculum as because the assistance given education was a means of coping with other national problems. Unemployment was an overriding concern, and many of the acts were devised to take care of those who would otherwise be idle. The Civilian Conservation Corps was designed for older youth and young people who had dropped out of school or who had recently graduated and who could find no employment in the labor market. Besides the work projects which dealt with some aspect of conservation, a program of training was provided with the goal of developing employable skills.

The National Youth Administration subsidized jobs devised by the schools, including assistance with the clerical work of teachers, so that students would be encouraged to remain in school. Adult education programs were assisted on a large scale, providing work for unemployed teachers and encouraging adults to employ wisely some of their leisure time. Most of the school construction undertaken received federal financial assistance as part of the program of public works designed to stimulate employment. The Public Works Administration and the Works Progress Administration together spent over a billion dollars for school construction and school rehabilitation.

These depression-year programs were discontinued as economic conditions improved. Other programs have been established from time to time, however, as the result of national pressures only indirectly related to education. An example is the school lunch program. Activated largely as one means of dealing with huge farm surpluses, this program now expends over 100 million dollars a year. Although often classed as an aid to education, it is equally an aid to agriculture. Indeed, the National School Lunch Act is administered at the federal level by the Department of Agriculture.

In recent years programs somewhat similar to those of the depression years have been devised for those who are economically disadvantaged. The Economic Opportunity Act of 1964 establishes a Job Corps for youth sixteen through twenty-one years of age who are lacking in fundamental schooling and job skills. The statement of purpose of Title I, Part A, reads:

> The purpose of this part is to prepare for the responsibilities of citizenship and to increase the employability of young men and young women aged sixteen through twenty-one by providing them in rural and urban residential centers with education, vocational training, useful work experience, including work directed toward the conservation of natural resources and other appropriate activities.[4]

Some of the residential centers will be established where the work activity of the corpsmen can be devoted to the conservation of natural resources and the improvement of public recreational areas. Those in these camps will be members of the Youth Conservation Corps, a subdivision of the Job Corps. The rural residential centers will be operated directly under the Office of Economic Opportunity.

Some centers will be located in unused federal facilities in metropolitan areas; some may be operated under contract with universities, public school systems, or corporations. The emphasis will be on a coordinated residential program of basic education, vocational training, and constructive work experience.

Part B of Title I (the Neighborhood Youth Corps) provides part-time or full-time work experience for young men and young women drawn largely from the ranks of the unemployed. They will be assigned work in settlement houses, parks and playgrounds, schools, libraries, and hospitals. This work experience is intended

---

[4] Public Law 88-452, The Economic Opportunity Act of 1964, Title I—Youth Programs, Part A—Job Corps.

to improve their employability in similar jobs on a permanent basis or else to provide the funds enabling them either to stay in school or to return to school.

Part B of Title II grants federal funds to states in which local educational agencies set up special programs of literacy instruction. Emphasis will be on assisting those who have an employability handicap because of insufficient mastery of oral or written language by an adult basic education program for persons with less than a sixth grade education.

The Manpower Development and Training Act of 1962 authorizes specialized vocational training programs for the unemployed and underemployed. The particular fields in which training or retraining is provided in any given geographic area are determined by labor surveys, so that there are placement opportunities for those who complete an intensive training program. On-the-job training is authorized as well as regular classes conducted by public and private institutions. Subsistence and training allowances are provided for those who meet certain qualifications.

It is significant to note that recently enacted programs, like those in the depression years, are not the administrative responsibility of the Office of Education and that some of these training programs are conducted entirely apart from any relationship with the public schools.

Assistance to federally impacted school districts. Whenever the federal government through some action on its part creates conditions which impose a hardship on local school districts, federal assistance of some type is likely to be forthcoming. During World War II large military installations were brought into being overnight. Dependents of men assigned to these installations swarmed into schools incapable of dealing with such sudden increases in enrollment. Nor did these school districts have sufficient tax resources to extend their programs and erect new school buildings. The same situation also appeared in many communities in which large defense plants were built or expanded—often with government funds and exempt from taxation. Federal aid was given these communities under the Lanham Act, the amount of aid being directly proportional to the influx of children whose parents were employed in national defense activities. This principle was extended in postwar years when Public Laws 815 and 874, passed in 1950, provided for federal aid both for school construction and school operation when the local district could establish that it was an "impacted area" due to federal activity.

Public Laws 815 and 874 were established as measures to provide temporary aid, and it was expected that they would pass out of existence after assisting seriously overburdened school districts. However, the percentage of "federally connected" pupils that a district must have in order to qualify for assistance is relatively small—generally 3 per cent in small communities and 6 per cent in larger cities—and many districts have now qualified for benefits under this act. Every state has school districts which participate in this aid.

> Approximately 4,100 school districts qualify for aid under the federally impacted programs. They enroll about 11 million children, or about one-third of all public elementary and secondary school students in the United States. Of these students, approximately 1.7 million are termed "federally connected."[5]

Since 1950 more than a billion dollars has been provided for school construction under Public Law 815. An even larger sum has been appropriated to assist in the operating expenses of the schools under Public Law 874.

The National Defense Education Act. Public Law 85–864, the Hill-Elliott Act, was signed into law by President Eisenhower on September 2, 1958. It is better known as the National Defense Education Act. The title is a proper one as the act was the response of Congress to the jitters and fears produced by Sputnik. It is a recognition that a strengthened educational program is necessary to national defense and survival.

The National Defense Education Act represents a "broken front" approach to the problems facing education. It does not seek to improve education "across the board," but provides stimulative grants designed to encourage and to strengthen particular elements in the school program.

The NDEA is an omnibus act which groups together somewhat unrelated provisions. The eleven titles in the act touch upon educational problems from the elementary grades through the grad-

---

[5] Committee on Education and Labor, House of Representatives, Eighty-Eighth Congress, First Session, *The Federal Government and Education.* Committee Print. Washington: U.S. Government Printing Office, 1963, p. 63.

uate school.[6] Less than half of the titles provide funds for public elementary and secondary schools. The other titles are important, dealing with loans for undergraduate college students, fellowships for graduate students, teacher preparation institutes, the establishment and operation of modern foreign language centers, and the inauguration of a Science Information Service. This discussion will concern itself with those provisions of the act that have a direct bearing on elementary and secondary programs.

Title III as adopted in 1958 has as its goal the improvement of instruction in science, mathematics, and modern foreign languages. The largest share of funds authorized in this title are grants to schools for the purchase of laboratory or other special equipment. Minor remodeling of the physical plant to provide for better laboratories is also included in this title.

One provision in Title III sets aside 12 per cent of the available funds appropriated for instructional equipment to be used as loans for the purchase of equipment by the private schools in each state. Each state shares in the amount thus set aside according to the percentage its private school enrollment is of the private school enrollment in the country as a whole. Loans bear interest one-quarter of 1 per cent in excess of the interest on outstanding marketable obligations of the United States and must be repaid within a ten year period.

The National Defense Education Act has had several extensions, often with increased appropriations. When it was extended by the Eighty-Eighth Congress in 1963 and 1964, English, reading, history, geography, civics, test grading equipment, and audio-visual library equipment were added to the fields and services for which equipment funds could be used.

Title III of the act also authorizes appropriations to be paid to state educational agencies for the improvement and expansion of their consultant services to elementary and secondary schools in the same fields in which equipment procurement is authorized. It is hoped that the assistance which may be given teachers on the job by state consultants may result in a substantial upgrading of the quality of instruction.

---

[6] There were ten titles in the bill originally enacted in 1958. The eleventh title was added in 1964 and provides for an expansion of teachers institutes at colleges and universities.

Title V has as its goal the establishment of better guidance programs in the schools of the nation. Provision for the statewide testing of pupils with the goal of determining their capacities and abilities and of identifying those with outstanding aptitudes must be included in the state plan for guidance services submitted in order to gain federal funds. Students are to be advised as to which courses are best suited to their talents. Outstandingly able students are to be encouraged to take courses which will prepare them for college entrance.

This testing program is to involve non-public as well as public school pupils. When a state's legal structure does not permit the state agency to do this, the U.S. Commissioner of Education arranges with the private schools for the testing program; the private schools, however, pay the sums which would normally be paid by state matching.

The guidance functions supported under Title V were originally confined to the high school. In 1964 this title was modified so that assistance is extended downward to the elementary schools and upward to include public junior colleges and technical institutes.

Title VII underwrites research grants and negotiated contracts designed to obtain answers as to how the varied audio-visual media may best be used. The title calls for "experimentation in the development and evaluation of projects involving television, radio, motion pictures, and related media of communication."[7] The U.S. Commissioner of Education is assisted in the administration of this title by a fourteen member Advisory Committee on New Educational Media which makes recommendations concerning the research program. There is provision for dissemination of the research findings and for assistance to state and local educational agencies in the more effective use of audio-visual aids.

Title VIII provides grants to schools for area vocational school programs. This title is really an amendment of the George-Barden Act relating to vocational education. Title VIII in turn has been subsumed under the broader provisions of the Vocational Education Act of 1963.

Title X stresses the need for improving the data-collecting function of state education departments. While the United States Office

---

[7] Public Law, 85-864, The National Defense Education Act of 1958.

of Education assembles data on a national scale concerning many facts of school status and operation, these facts, because of our decentralized school system, must first be gathered in each of the states. Many of the state departments are understaffed, modern machine methods of codifying data are not always employed, and definitions of terms under which data are collected are not standardized. National statistics are no better than the sources from which they are derived. This title of the act seeks prompt and accurate reporting from the various states.

The pattern generally followed in those sections of the National Defense Education Act which pertain to elementary and secondary schools is that a state plan is presented which shows that federal money will be used in accordance with the intent of the Act and that defensible criteria will be followed in determining the priority of the various projects for which local school districts seek aid. Federal funds must be matched on a fifty-fifty basis.

The National Defense Education Act as enacted in 1958 provided for contracts with colleges and universities for training counselors (Title V–B) and for establishing institutes in which prospective language teachers and teachers in service could become better qualified for teaching modern languages in the elementary and secondary schools (Title VI).

Under Title XI, enacted in 1964, these training institutes were extended to include teachers or supervisors in reading, history, geography, and English. Training institutes were also established for teachers of disadvantaged youth, school library personnel, and educational media specialists.[8] Federal funds underwrite the costs of the institutes under contracts with colleges and enrollees receive subsistence benefits; no tuition is charged.

At the end of the first year of the operation of the National Defense Education Act, Lawrence G. Derthick, then U.S. Commissioner of Education, gave his appraisal of this legislation:

> It does not solve all of today's educational problems, yet never before in the Nation's history has there been so comprehensive a program of federal assistance to strengthen education at critical points from the elementary grades through the graduate school.[9]

---

[8] Public Law 88–665, National Defense Education Act Amended, 1964.
[9] Lawrence G. Derthick, "Box Score on the National Defense Education Act," *NEA Journal*, XLVIII (September 1959), 37.

This opinion might not prevail today. In 1963 President Johnson termed the Higher Education Facilities Act "the most significant education bill passed by Congress in the history of the Republic," and legislation passed since that time eclipses both of these acts.[10] Still, the National Defense Education Act is important in the annals of American education. It foreshadowed the widespread involvement of the federal government in many different aspects of the country's educational program.

The Elementary and Secondary Education Act of 1965. The act of greatest impact on elementary and secondary education to date is Public Law 89–10, more familiarly known as the Elementary and Secondary Education Act of 1965. This is an omnibus act covering a variety of programs. Every school district and every school pupil will feel the influence of this act, at least in some measure. More than a billion dollars were authorized under this act for the fiscal year 1966, although slightly less than that amount was actually appropriated by Congress for the first year of operation. Additional funds are projected for succeeding fiscal years.

More than three-quarters of the funds are to be distributed under Title I of the act. This title can be characterized as part of the "war on poverty," and is designed to assist children who have been educationally deprived because of economic or cultural factors. It has been estimated that as many as nine of every ten school districts will receive some funds under Title I.

The amount which may be available to a given school district is determined by a formula which starts with the number of school-age children in the district who come from families with annual incomes of less than $2,000. Children from families who receive more than $2,000 a year from the program of Aid to Families with Dependent Children are also counted. The number of these children is then multiplied by one-half of the average annual current expenditure per pupil in the state in which the district is located. Although these figures are specified for the first year of operation, Congress has reserved to itself the renewal or modification of the formula. It can determine whether the $2,000 specified as the low income factor shall be changed and whether the percentage of current expenditure

---

[10] The quotation of President Johnson's remarks is taken from comments made by the president when signing H.R. 6143, the Higher Education Facilities Act of 1963. White House release, December 16, 1963, p. 1.

per pupil in the formula, termed the "federal participation," shall remain at 50 per cent.

A school district must have a minimum number of children whose families qualify as low-income families before it is eligible for federal funds. The number of children must be at least 100 or must be at least 3 per cent of the total number of children in the district between the ages of five and seventeen. Under the latter stipulation, the 3 per cent must include at least ten children.

While the formula for determining the distribution of federal monies is based on economic deprivation, the programs to be mounted under Title I may be designed to overcome any form of educational disadvantage. The physically handicapped and the mentally retarded as well as those who are culturally deprived may be included in the programs which are devised. Each local educational agency formulates its own plans subject to state approval. Two or more districts may combine to arrange a more comprehensive program. Variations in plans are encouraged so that the needs of each district can be met. Some of the suggestions which have been advanced by the United States Office of Education in describing the operation of Title I include special classes, remedial teachers, guidance services, provisions for liaison with the home and with community agencies, curriculum materials centers which develop instructional units and materials for the disadvantaged including programmed materials and audio-visual aids, educational radio and television programs, mobile services and equipment carried to individual schools, and field trips for cultural and educational development. Expenditures may be made for additional personnel, for equipment, and for new curricular materials and techniques.

Title I contains a new departure in federal aid to elementary and secondary schools in that services to disadvantaged children are to be extended to children in non-public as well as in public schools. The control of funds expended and the title to equipment must remain with the public agency, but the act does mandate that special educational services designed to overcome disadvantage—such as educational radio and television programs, media centers, and mobile educational services and equipment—are to be made available to non-public school pupils. The possibility of dual enrollment is specifically mentioned.

Federal funds for Title I are funneled through the state educational agency, but the state must certify to the federal government that programs are directed toward the amelioration and elimination of educational deprivation, that the special services rendered are being made available to non-public school pupils as well as to public school children with a public agency administering all funds and property, that procedures have been developed to evaluate the programs undertaken with provision for dissemination of promising practices, and that services and projects are dovetailed with community action programs in those communities having such programs under the Economic Opportunity Act.

Title II of the Act recognizes the inadequacies which prevail with respect to instructional materials in many school systems and provides funds to make library books, textbooks, audio-visual aids, and other instructional materials available to pupils and teachers. It has been pointed out that nearly a third of all school children attend schools in which there is no library. The proportion is higher for pupils in elementary schools. Many textbooks are outdated; inadequate provision is made in many systems for audio-visual aids.

A state plan is drawn up for the utilization of federal funds. In allocating funds or materials to school districts, the state is to develop criteria which assess the relative need for such materials. Books and materials provided must not supplant the materials being furnished by the local districts; the intent is to insure that better provision of instructional resources extends learning opportunities.

Materials made available to non-public school pupils are on a loan basis and do not become the property of the non-public school. In those states in which legal restrictions prevent such an arrangement, the U.S. Commissioner of Education is authorized to make available to non-public schools materials comparable to those being distributed by the state agency.

Under Title III, federal assistance is available to local educational agencies or combinations of school districts to establish what are called "Supplementary Educational Centers and Services." The intent is to provide a wide variety of educational services on a community or regional basis to both public and private schools so that the programs of all schools in the area are enriched. Stress is placed on educational innovations which give promise of improving instruction.

This is the most comprehensive title in the act and leaves a great deal of discretion to local authorities. Illustrative of the services which might be rendered are remedial teachers, school health services, guidance and counseling, curriculum laboratory services, and radio and television programs. School museums may be established. The cultural resources which might be utilized in the community—with financial assistance to make them more fully possible—include symphony concerts, dramatic productions, presentations by artists and musicians. Advanced placement programs and specialized instruction in advanced courses are encouraged. Money for necessary capital expenditures may be allocated. Mobile science and language laboratories and bookmobiles are possible.

Applications for funds under Title III are made to the U.S. Office of Education, but all applications must be reviewed by the state educational agency to insure that the state's allotment will be used efficiently. A local school district must utilize the educational resources and agencies available to it in planning and carrying out a proposed program. Such agencies could include colleges and universities, non-profit private schools, libraries and museums, artistic and musical organizations, and educational radio and television stations.

An important provision of Title IV calls for the establishment of educational laboratories with research, demonstration, dissemination, and service functions. A laboratory is organized as a consortium of colleges and universities, school systems, state departments of education, and possibly other public and private agencies. Most laboratories will be based on and will serve a region of several states. It is intended that funds to support laboratories will be expended in such a fashion that no part of the country will be excluded from participation in a regional educational laboratory. Many different types of educational problems will be tackled by the regional laboratories, and the attack is expected to be a multi-disciplinary one. It is intended that the regional laboratory will serve education somewhat as the agricultural experiment station serves agriculture.

The guidelines for the administration of Title IV state that:

> Laboratories will conduct a wide range of research, development, and dissemination programs including basic and applied research, curriculum development and evaluation, development of promising

innovations, demonstrations of noteworthy programs and practices, training and dissemination activities, research information centers, and consultation services to assist schools in the implementation of educational improvements developed through research.[11]

Besides inaugurating educational laboratories, Title IV continues and expands the research and development activities of the Cooperative Research Program.

Title V provides funds to strengthen state departments of education in such basic activities as data-gathering, statewide planning, curriculum development, consultative services to school districts, and appraisal and evaluation. Much of the money will probably be spent to increase the staffing of state departments with qualified personnel.

The wide-ranging provisions of the Elementary and Secondary Education Act of 1965 represent a departure in many respects from previous federal legislation. More communities and more pupils are affected than ever before. Continuing federal support is anticipated; this is no stopgap measure. Federal funds are being used to support services and to purchase materials for the use of children in nonpublic schools; the child-benefit theory has been broadly extended. More than ever before, aspects of the curriculum will be probed with the support of federal funds. A great deal of latitude is given local communities in the nature of the activities they propose to meet the objectives of the act. Emphasis is placed on research, experimentation, innovation, and evaluation.

Summary of the Role of the Federal Government

A complete catalog of all federal legislation affecting American education would fill many monographs. This chapter has highlighted the more important federal aid measures affecting elementary and secondary schools passed by Congress. If an effort is made to generalize the role the federal government has played, these statements seem supportable:

1. Although education is primarily a state function, there has always been concern on the national level that each state assume

---

[11] Office of Education, *Guidelines for a National Program of Educational Laboratories,* Public Law 89–10, Title IV. Washington: Office of Education, U.S. Department of Health, Education, and Welfare, 1965, p. 2 (mimeographed statement).

its function of providing an adequate educational program. This concern was early shown in land grants for educational purposes and was voiced in the Northwest Ordinance: "the means of education shall forever be encouraged."[12]

2. Federal grants-in-aid have frequently been pointed toward a strengthening of those particular parts of the educational program which appear to have been lagging in terms of the national interest. The Smith-Hughes Act encouraging vocational education is a case in point.

3. Federal grants-in-aid have generally been stimulative in character. Matching of funds on the part of state or local authorities has often been a requirement.

4. Many of the federal programs which have entailed the greatest expenditures of money have been byproducts of pressing problems of national concern other than education, and not directly geared to the pressing problems of education. Aid for the construction of schools in the 1930s was sparked more by the problem of unemployment than by national concern over unsafe and outmoded school buildings. The educational programs of the Civilian Conservation Corps and the National Youth Administration were a direct consequence of the unemployment problem. The school lunch program seems motivated more by the problem of agricultural surpluses than by the nutritional needs of children, although no one would deny the contribution made by the school lunch program to better nutrition. The GI Bill responded to the pleas of veterans to provide for their postponed education and was associated with the possible effect on employment of rapid demobilization.

5. When the federal government through its actions creates conditions which place a hardship on local school districts, federal assistance is invoked. The "federally impacted areas" programs illustrate this point.

6. Varying degrees of conformity to specified conditions have accompanied federal grants-in-aid. There has been practically no interference by the federal government in the direct operation and administration of instruction in the states and in the local school districts, however. States and school districts have been free to de-

---

[12] Ordinance of 1787 establishing policies for the Northwest Territory.

termine whether they wish to meet the qualifications for any specific grant-in-aid.

7. Pressures for federal action mount when a void is created in which the efforts of state school authorities seem inadequate to meet some particular problem. CCC programs would probably not have been instituted in the depression years if state school systems had met the problems of the school drop-out, the untrained worker, the youth who longed for an outdoor-living experience associated with constructive work activity while obtaining educational upgrading. This is true also of the factors which led to today's Job Corps.

8. Federal programs have been developed on a piecemeal basis, and there has been no over-all coordination. Many programs are sponsored and directed by federal agencies other than the Office of Education.

9. The federal government up to the present time has not accepted the role of financial participation with state and local school districts to assure sufficient funds for a foundation program so that each child is certain of at least a minimum level of educational opportunity. The financial assistance given by the federal government may be characterized as a broken-front approach, assisting certain aspects of the schools' program which appear to be lagging and which seem at any given time to be particularly crucial.

Pros and Cons of Federal Aid to Education

With a long history of federal financial assistance of various types and with more than a billion dollars a year now being spent for direct support of the educational system of the United States, it is often stated that it is not a question of whether there should be federal aid but a question of the kind and amount of federal assistance to be provided. Still, the issue of whether the federal government has a legitimate role to play in the financing of education is a controversial one—as attested by the volumes of testimony and debate presented in every congressional session. This chapter would be incomplete without reference to the fundamental issue: should there be federal aid to education?

The pros of this question may be enumerated as follows:

1. Each child is entitled to an opportunity for at least a minimum program of education regardless of place of birth or residence

FEDERAL GOVERNMENT FINANCING EDUCATION 103

or the wealth of the state in which he resides. A federal assistance program can contain an equalization factor so that poorer states will receive greater aid. The motivating purpose behind federal aid should be the guaranteeing of a minimum level of educational opportunity to each child. The country should not stand by content with letting a poor state do the best it can if its minimum efforts are grossly inadequate.

2. Our national security and welfare demand an educated and a productive citizenry. The United States cannot maintain a position of pre-eminence with only 7 per cent of the population of the world and 6 per cent of the land surface unless it utilizes to the utmost the potentialities of every person. Each person must have the fullest opportunity to progress to the highest levels which his abilities and interests permit, not only because this is a basic tenet of democracy, but also because it is necessary if the United States is to survive as a world power.

3. The population increase has produced demands for classrooms and teachers that school systems have been unable to fulfill. For more than ten years schools have opened each fall with a shortage of more than 100,000 classrooms. While the shortage is being slowly whittled away, the backlog of classroom needs that goes back to World War II has not been reduced substantially. The number of teachers with substandard certificates has changed little in the last decade and remains at around 80,000.

4. Federal aid taps the resources of the entire country in behalf of education. Two-thirds of all taxes collected are collected at the federal level. The federal government constitutes a single tax jurisdiction unhampered by the vying between states that frequently goes on in connection with state taxes as each state seeks competitively to provide a more favorable climate for industry. Federal taxes reflect ability to pay more nearly than do state or local taxes, and federal tax revenues respond quickly to changes in the economy.

5. Federal resources have not been tapped as heavily as state and local resources in terms of the potential that exists. The rate of tax increase in the last fifteen years has been more steep at state and local levels than at the federal level. Local and state debt combined has been increasing more than twenty times as fast as the federal debt in recent years.

6. The federal tax collection machinery is the most efficient of

all the tax collection mechanisms, while the cost of collection and administration of local taxes is the most expensive. State taxes are collected more efficiently than local taxes but not at as low a rate per $1,000 collected as federal taxes.

7. The growing population mobility in the United States demands greater equalization of educational programs. More than a million young people between the ages of five and seventeen move from one state to another each year. It has been said that "ignorance, like disease, knows no boundaries."

8. We are spending millions abroad through foreign aid in behalf of the educational programs of newly developing countries. The educational welfare of our own children is at least equally important.

9. Substantial federal assistance has been provided for programs involving agriculture, highways, housing, hospitals, and public health. Of the most pressing domestic concerns, only education receives as little as 8 per cent assistance from the federal government.

10. There is a 180-year history of federal interest in education dating back to the days of the land grants. Federal assistance has been provided local school systems in a variety of ways and has been invoked when local and state efforts have proved inadequate in meeting critical needs. This assistance has been accomplished without interference in the administration of the schools.

On the con side of the federal aid question are these arguments:

1. Education is a state function and not a national responsibility. There exists no express constitutional provision for the federal government to assume any type of responsibility for education. Federal assistance to date has not been directed to the general support of elementary and secondary schools, but has had as its goal other primary objectives such as the relief of unemployment, the promotion of agriculture, or the requirements of national defense.

2. Federal aid takes away local initiative and leads ultimately to federal control. Even though bills before Congress contain prohibitions against federal interference in matters of curriculum or administration, any aid granted will operate as a foot in the door, with higher appropriations later being demanded and with controls ultimately creeping in. The person who pays the piper calls the tune.

3. The country cannot afford to underwrite education at the national level. The federal budget should be reduced, not raised. The

federal debt is now more than four times the size of the combined state and local debt. If some of the taxpaying capacity which the federal government has pre-empted were to be returned to the states, the states would be in a position to take care of their own programs of education.

4. Public school expenditures have been increasing at a rate which exceeds the rate of increase in public school enrollments. The most critical stage of population increase has been passed. The rate of growth in public elementary and secondary schools is decreasing.

5. Under federal programs with an equalization factor, more taxes will be drawn from wealthy states than will be returned to these states for the partial subsidization of their educational programs. It is unrealistic to expect the wealthier states to support such a program before they have had a chance to put their own schools in good order.

6. Federal aid with federal control is not generally advocated. Federal aid without federal control could lead to the perpetuation of undesirable educational practices—for example, the perpetuation of unsatisfactory school districts.

7. Under a federal aid program there will be administrative costs in the processing of tax collections in Washington and in the distribution of funds for education to the various states—the "freight cost" in sending money to Washington and back again. These costs will be avoided if the states themselves take care of their own levies for education.

8. Private and parochial schools may not participate in substantial measure in a general aid federal support program for public schools. Parents who exercise religious freedom by sending their children to church-linked schools are penalized by the exclusion of these schools from federal funds. Parents who send their children to private schools can hardly be expected to tax themselves more heavily than they are now taxed for the education of children not their own.

9. States and local communities can be aided by federal grants to other governmental agencies where the threat of federal control may not be as serious. If states are given federal assistance for the building of roads and hospitals, for unemployment insurance, and for social security, then, since the states will not need to make as

large levies for these purposes, tax leeway will be created whereby the states may give increased support to schools.

10. The public schools can be financed adequately from state and local revenue sources. School programs are improving with every passing year. The level of teacher preparation is increasing as are teachers salaries. District reorganizations are bringing about educational efficiency. More than 60,000 classrooms are being built each year. Growth in educational expenditures has exceeded increases in corporate profits and in living standards as measured by per capital expenditures for personal consumption. Educational progress is not on a plateau from which the schools must be rescued by federal intervention.

There are other arguments sometimes set forth, but those listed above are the ones presented with the greatest frequency. There has been no attempt to evaluate them; parallel arguments are sometimes found on opposite sides of the issue. Some of the arguments are inconsistent—for example, the argument that federal aid leads to federal control conflicts with the argument that federal aid without control perpetuates undesirable educational practices. Still, the arguments, both pro and con, are presented forcefully in committee rooms and on the legislative floor with every passing year.

Ancillary Issues Concerning Federal Aid

There are a number of subsidiary issues which accompany the question of federal assistance. Reference has been made to some of them in the pros and cons enumerated above.

The question of whether federal aid can be distributed without controls which go beyond the accounting function necessary to determine that money is being spent for the purposes appropriated receives much discussion. General aid bills contain some such phrase as this:

> In the administration of this Act, no department, agency, officer or employee of the United States shall exercise any direction, supervision, or control over policy determination, personnel, curriculum, program of instruction, or the administration of any school or school system.[13]

---

[13] Section 11 of S–2, Eighty-Sixth Congress, 1st Session, the Murray-Metcalf Bill.

The largest federal expenditure for education to date has been the GI Bill in which controls were at a minimum with $14.5 billion being distributed. On the other hand, federal grants for vocational education have generally been prescriptive as to their use, and state plans approved by the federal government have preceded the release of state allocations. An element in a state plan not in harmony with federal policies must be modified or stricken.

One of the safeguards against federal interference is a provision that federal funds for local school districts be channeled through the state educational agency. Direct assistance to local school districts by the federal government, bypassing the state office of education, invites the imposition of federal controls.

A very live issue is that of categorical grants versus general support—that is, whether federal aid should be designed primarily to meet stress situations (such as a shortage of classrooms or a lag in science teaching) or whether it should be long-range general support unassociated with particular aspects of the school's program.

Federal assistance to date can be characterized as a "broken-front" approach attempting to deal with the most important pressures of the moment. The rationale for categorical grants is that the function of federal assistance is to meet needs of high priority, to balance the serious gaps, and to place the federal government in a leadership role whereby stimulus is given to new and experimental programs. Categorical aid is often viewed as being temporary. When the gap the aid seeks to overcome is eliminated, federal aid for this particular purpose can be removed. Thus in his message on education delivered in January 1963, President Kennedy stated that federal participation "should be selective, stimulative, and, where possible, temporary."[14]

In contrast to the broken-front approach of stimulative aids and measures is the concept that federal assistance should be a long-range commitment to the underwriting of general school operations. Such a commitment is urged on the grounds that the federal government has a legitimate and vital financial stake in education. It is argued that federal monies can be more efficiently spent if the exact determination of the purposes for which they are spent is left to the states and the communities. The priorities in one community

---

[14] John F. Kennedy, "Message on Education," January 29, 1963. Text appearing in Charles A. Quattlebaum, *op. cit.*, p. 132.

may differ from the priorities in another. There is less likelihood of any federal control being possible when federal funds are merged with state and local funds with the primary goal of providing a satisfactory level of education in all communities. Overhead costs of administration of the assistance program at the federal level are kept at a minimum since there are no state plans to approve and since the distribution of funds can be made on the basis of a simple, objective formula with a single payment being made to each state. Large additions to staffs of state departments of education are not needed to administer this sort of federal program.

The rationale underlying the concept of general federal support is that the major need to be met in education is the availability of an amount per pupil in each school district which will make possible a satisfactory educational program. It is contended that it is the lack of sufficient financing which has created the gaps now faced in education. The remedy is not merely to erase the gaps through special aids, for other gaps will occur as civilization progresses and the needs of education change. The remedy is to provide a floor level of financing which will make it possible for every school district to provide at least a minimum level of educational opportunity. With financial capability, it is presumed that school districts will spend the monies available to them wisely. The remedy for inefficiency or abuse, should such occur, would be the relentless glare of publicity rather than any type of federal supervision or control.

The National Education Association and the American Association of School Administrators are two of the organizations which have strongly advocated general aid to education. The Educational Policies Commission, a joint advisory commission created by these two bodies, similarly held this point of view, at least until 1964. Then, after summarizing the drawbacks of categorical aid in a publication entitled *Educational Responsibilities of the Federal Government,* the Commission came to the conclusion that in the immediate future general aid, although still a goal to be sought, was not likely to be realized. The Commission called for exploration of alternatives.

> In view of the failure of the Congress to establish general nationwide federal aid to education, and in view of the actual existence of a number of categorical aids, we recommend that educational leadership devote immediate and detailed attention to the improvement

and spread of categorical aids, in order to obtain, to the extent possible, the values previously sought through general aid.[15]

Thus, the Commission advocates the extension of grants aiding particular subjects to more of the subjects in the curriculum and to more educational services. This goal has already been partially accomplished in the 1964 extensions of the National Defense Education Act and in the Elementary and Secondary Education Act of 1965. The Commission states:

> Of every existing or new proposal, educators and federal policymakers should ask how it may be made to (a) put more money into serving (b) more categories and (c) lower levels.[16]

In recent years two other issues have been stumbling blocks to federal aid legislation: the issue of barring federal aid to segregated schools and the issue of federal funds for parochial as well as for public schools. The first of these has been resolved by the passing of the Civil Rights Act of 1964. Under this act recipients of federal aid are required to file statements that there will be no discrimination in the programs for which funds are being received. Regulations published in connection with the administration of the act provide for procedures to be followed, with ultimate recourse to judicial review, when discrimination is alleged.

The issue of using tax funds to support non-public schools was discussed as Issue 6 in Chapter IV.[17] Here the question revolved about the inclusion of non-public schools in state assistance programs, but the same arguments have echoed in the halls of Congress in connection with federal legislation. The Elementary and Secondary Education Act of 1965 and the provisions it makes for assistance to non-public school pupils have been outlined. It was thought that this act could not have been passed, for practical political reasons, unless some services were extended to non-public schools. It would appear that the line of separation between church and state has at least been blurred, and there is a likelihood that a whole new series of questions will be raised about tax support for private schools. Some contend that everything that is not strictly sectarian

---
[15] Educational Policies Commission, *Educational Responsibilities of the Federal Government*. Washington: National Education Association, 1964, p. 18.
[16] *Ibid.*, p. 19.
[17] *Supra*, pp. 52–56.

could ultimately be construed as "child-benefit" rather than church assistance.

The provisions of this act are likely to be tested in the courts. Perhaps guidelines will be established ultimately by court decisions which will remove the church-state issue from the arena in which federal assistance to schools is debated.

The entry of the Elementary and Secondary Education Act of 1965 into a broad spectrum of educational activity may stall a drive toward general, unearmarked federal aid to education. The multiplying of federal grants will achieve some of the effect of general aid that was advocated by the Educational Policies Commission, but this could be at the expense of heavy administrative costs, lack of coordination among federal programs administered by a variety of agencies, the risk of federal controls, and inflexibility in the administration of funds at the local level.

It is apparent that what is happening on the national scene is akin to the period through which state school financing passed some thirty or forty years ago. Grants for special purposes were increased until the structure of state supervision, manifold reports, and matching demands became so inflexible and top-heavy that reforms seemed imperative. A foundation program was substituted for many of the special aids in a large number of states. Perhaps the nation as a whole must pass through such a period before a simple structure of general aid can be erected at the federal level.

In any case, it is apparent that there is a growing opinion that local and state financing of public education must be reinforced by national support. Education is emerging not just as a state-local partnership but as a state-local-federal partnership.

Bibliography

Barr, W. Monfort, *American Public School Finance.* New York: American Book Co., 1960.

Benson, Charles S., *The Economics of Public Education.* Boston: Houghton Mifflin Co., 1961.

———, *Perspectives on the Economics of Education, Readings, in School Finance and Business Management.* Boston: Houghton Mifflin Co., 1963.

Burke, Arvid J., *Financing Public Schools in the United States.* rev. ed. New York: Harper & Row, Publishers, 1957.

Burkhead, Jesse, *State and Local Taxes for Public Education.* Syracuse: Syracuse University Press, 1963.

Chamber of Commerce of the United States, *Education—An Investment in People.* 3rd ed. Washington, D.C.: Chamber of Commerce of the United States, 1964.

Committee on Educational Finance, *New Local Sources of Tax Revenues.* Washington, D.C.: National Education Association, 1959.

Committee on Tax Education and School Finance, *Action in State Equalization: Case Studies.* Washington, D.C.: National Education Association, 1959.

———, *Does Better Education Cost More?* Washington, D.C.: National Education Association, 1959.

———, *Equalization of Property Assessments.* Washington, D.C.: National Education Association, 1958.

———, *Guides—To the Improvement of State School Finance Programs.* Washington, D.C.: National Education Association, 1958.

Corbally, John E., Jr., *School Finance.* Boston: Allyn and Bacon, Inc., 1962.

Educational Policies Commission, *National Policy and the Financing of the Public Schools.* Washington, D.C.: National Education Association, 1959.

Groves, Harold M., *Education and Economic Growth.* Washington, D.C.: The Committee on Educational Finance, National Education Association, 1961.

Innes, Jon T., Paul B. Jacobson, and Roland J. Pellegrin, *The Economic Returns to Education, A Survey of the Findings.* Eugene, Oregon: The Center for the Advanced Study of Educational Administration, University of Oregon, 1965.

Johns, Roe L., and Edgar L. Morphet, *Financing the Public Schools.* Englewood Cliffs, N.J.: Prentice-Hall, Inc., 1960.

Johns, Roe L., and Edgar L. Morphet, eds., *Problems and Issues in Public School Finance*. New York: National Conference of Professors of Educational Administration, Teachers College, Columbia University, 1952.

Lindman, Erick L., *The Federal Government and Public Schools*. Washington, D.C.: The American Association of School Administrators, 1965.

Mort, Paul R., Walter C. Ruesser, and John W. Polley, *Public School Finance, Its Background, Structure and Operation*. New York: McGraw Hill Book Co., Inc., 1960.

Munger, Frank J., and Richard F. Fenno, Jr., *National Politics and Federal Aid to Education*. Syracuse: Syracuse University Press, 1962.

Norton, John K., *Changing Demands on Education and Their Fiscal Implications*. Washington, D.C.: National Committee for the Support of the Public Schools, 1963.

Rosenstengel, William Everett, and Jefferson N. Eastmond, *School Finance, Its Theory and Practice*. New York: The Ronald Press Co., 1957.

Sufrin, Sidney C., *Issues in Federal Aid to Education*. Syracuse: Syracuse University Press, 1962.

Index

A

Adequacy, principle of, 35
Administration, percentage of expenditures for, 4
Alabama, 34, 72
Alaska, 86
American Association of School Administrators, 108
American Economic Review, 12n
Arkansas, 61
Armstrong, Herbert C., 74
Assessment of property, 33, 62–66 (*see also* Property, assessment)
Assessors, 33, 62–65

B

Barr, W. Monfort, 61, 71n
Benson, Charles S., 76
Birth rate trends, 7
Bretsch, Howard S., v
Budget hearings, 68
Burke, Arvid J., 50n
Burkhead, Jesse, 60, 65n, 72, 76, 78

C

Capital outlay, 3–4
Categorical grants v. general support, 107–109
Central Michigan School Administrators' Research Association, 79
Charge-financed services, 59
Child-benefit theory, 53, 100, 109–110
Civilian Conservation Corps, 89, 101, 102
Civil Rights Act of 1964, 109
Classroom shortage, 8, 103
Collection of property taxes, 70–71
Committee on Education and Labor, 92n
Connecticut, 63, 79–80, 82
Constitution:
  Constitutional Convention, 85
  First Amendment, 52–53, 55
  Tenth Amendment, 85
Continental Congress, 85
Contingency fund, 51–52
Corbally, John E., Jr., 19–20, 34, 46
Cooperative Research Program, 100
Cost-quality relation, 15–18

Costs of education, 1–4
  comparisons, 1900–1958, 2–3
  comparisons, 1949–50 to 1965–66 (*table*), 2
  distribution of expenditures by account headings (*figure*), 3, (*table*), 4
  expenditures per pupil (*table*), 2, 23–26

D

Delaware, 59, 63
Depression programs, 89–90
Derthick, Lawrence G., 95
Desegregation, 109
Distressed school districts, 51–52
Duplication of taxes, 73, 79, 83–84

E

Earmarked taxes, 80–81
Eastmond, Jefferson N., 44
Economic capacity to support education, 9–11
Economic indexes in mandatory local effort, 33–34
Economic Opportunity Act, 90, 98
Economy:
  growth of, 9–10
  school expenditures and, 9–14
Education:
  and economic development, 12–14
  an investment, 11–14
  outcomes of, 15
  non-monetary outcomes, 11
Education U.S.A., 17n
Educational Policies Commission, 20–27, 82n, 108–109
Elementary and Secondary Education Act of 1965, 56, 96–100, 109–110
Enrollments (*table*), 6, 6–8
Enrollment projections, 6–7
Equalization aid, 43–48, 66
  general purpose, 81
  special purpose, 81
Equalized valuation, 66
Everson v. Board of Education, 53, 56
Exemptions from taxation, 60–61, 64–65
Expenditures for education, 1–4 (*see also* Costs of education)

INDEX

F

Factors of production, 12
Farner, Frank, 74
Federally impacted school districts, 91–92, 101
Federal participation, 85–110
  arguments against, 104–106
  arguments for, 102–104
  depression measures, 89–91
  Elementary and Secondary Education Act of 1965, 96–100
  federal control, 104, 106–107
  federally impacted school districts, 91–92
  National Defense Education Act, 92–96
  role of federal government, 100–102
  vocational education, 86–88
Fiscal controls, 37–38, 57
Fiscally dependent school districts, 68–69 (*see also* School districts)
Fiscally independent school districts, 69 (*see also* School districts)
Fixed charges, percentage of expenditure for, 4
Flat grants, 43–48, 81
  general purpose, 81
  special purpose, 81
Foundation program, 18–27, 28–29
  appraisal of, 38–39
  classroom unit, 19–20
  comprehensiveness, 40–41
  determination of amount, 19–27
  expressed in dollar terms, 28–29
  mandatory local effort, 32–34, 36
  per pupil unit, 19
  proposal of Educational Policies Commission, 20–27
  sparsity recognition, 42
  state and local sharing, 30–32, 34–36
  tax leeway provided, 36–37
  urban area adjustment, 42–43

G

Galbraith, John K., 13
General aid:
  federal, 107–109
  state, 46–48
George-Barden Act, 87, 94
George-Dean Act, 87
George-Ellzey Act, 87
George-Reed Act, 87
G I Bill, 101, 107
Gifts and bequests, 59
Griffiths, Daniel E., vii
Gross national product:
  increase in, 9
  related to educational expenditures (*table*), 9, 10
Groves, Harold M., 13

H

Hawaii, 79, 86
Heller, Walter W., 11, 13
Hirsch, Werner A., 2, 3
Hobson, Carol Joy, 5n, 6n, 8n
Human capital, 12–14

I

Illinois, 54
Incentive aid, 48–50
Income tax, 78–79, 83–84
Indiana, 81
Installment paying of taxes, 70
Instruction, percentage of expenditures for, 4
Intangible personal property, 60–61 (*see also* Property)
Intermediate school districts, 25, 75 (*see also* School districts)
Internal Improvement Act of 1841, 80
Investment, education as an, 11

J

James, H. Thomas, 48, 51
Job Corps, 90, 102
Johns, Roe L., 81n
Johnson, Lyndon B., 96
The Journal of Political Economy, 13

K

Kennedy, John F., 87, 107
Kentucky, 86

L

Land grants, 79–80, 85–86, 101
Lanham Act, 91
Legislative appropriations, 81, 84
License fees, 79
Louisiana, 81

M

McClusky, Neil G., 55
Maine, 86
Mandatory local effort, 32–34

INDEX

Manpower Development and Training Act, 91
Maryland, 50
Matching funds and grants, 41, 56, 89, 101
Michigan, 29, 54
Millage rate, 32–34, 67, 69
  ceilings on, 69–70
Miller, Herman P., 11–12
Minnesota, 63
Mississippi, 82
Montana, 63
Mort, Paul R., 16n, 18n
Morphet, Edgar L., 37, 81n
Murray v. Curlett, 56

N

National Advisory Committee on School Finance, 52
National Defense Education Act, 92–96, 109
National Education Association, 2n, 108
  Committee on Educational Finance, 10, 31n, 78n
  Committee on Tax Education and School Finance, 39, 41n, 44, 61n, 62, 66
  Educational Policies Commission, 20–27, 82n, 108–109
  Legislative Commission, 11n
  National School Public Relations Association, 17n
  Research Division, 53n
National Youth Administration, 89, 101
Nebraska, 59
New Hampshire, 59
New Mexico, 59
New York, 61, 72
New York State Educational Conference Board, 50
Non-property taxes, local, 71–73
Non-public schools and tax support, 52–56, 109–110
Northwest Ordinance, 101
Norton, John K., 13–14

O

Objectivity in state support programs, 51–52
Office of Economic Opportunity, 90
Office of Education, 2n, 6, 88, 91, 94–95, 97, 99, 102
Ohio Legislative Service Commission, 63

P

Parochial schools, 52–56, 109–110 (*see also* Non-public schools and tax support)
Pennsylvania, 58, 61, 72
Permanent funds, 79–80, 84
Per pupil expenditures for education (*table*), 2, 23–26 (*see also* Costs of education)
Phi Delta Kappa, 52
Pierce, Truman M., 86
Plant maintenance, percentage of expenditures for, 4
Plant operation, percentage of expenditures for, 4
Polley, John W., 16n, 18n
Powell, Theodore, 53
Property:
  assessment, 33, 62–66
  assessment reforms, 63–66
  equalized evaluations, 66
  intangible personal property, 60–61
  real property, 60–61
  tangible personal property, 60
  taxable property, 60–61
  underassessment, 65
Property tax:
  collection, 70–71
  continuing yield, 76
  local, 58–71, 75–76
  millage levy, 67
  relief, 50–51
  state, 79, 84
  tax exemptions, 60–61, 65
Public laws 815 and 874, 91–92
Public Works Administration, 89
Pupil-staff ratio, 21–22

Q

Quality in education, measures of, 16–18
Quattlebaum, Charles A., 87n, 88

R

Real property, 60–61 (*see also* Property)
Regional educational laboratories, 99–100
Regressive taxes, 73, 77
Residual personal income, variations between states, 81–82
Reusser, Walter C., 16n, 18n

INDEX

Revenue:
  local revenue sources, 58–60
  state revenue sources, 77–80
    allocation to education, 80–81
    land grants, 79–80
    trends in, 83–84
    types of state tax, 78
  tax sources, federal, state, and local, 4 (*figure*), 5 (*table*), 31
  trends in tax sources, 4–5
Rhode Island, 50, 63
Rosenstengel, William E., 44
Rutledge, Mr. Justice, 56

S

Sales taxes, 77–78, 83
  general sales tax, 77–78
  on services, 83
  selective sales taxes, 77
Schloss, Samuel, 5n, 6n, 8n
School District of Abington Township, Pennsylvania v. Schempp, 56
School districts:
  fiscally dependent, 68–69
  fiscally independent, 69
  intermediate, 25, 75
  mandatory local effort, 32
  tax authorization, 58
  variation in wealth, 28
School district organization, 73–75
School lunch program, 42, 90, 101
Schultz, Theodore W., 13
Severance taxes, 79
Shared time, 53–54, 97
Simon, Kenneth A., 6n
Smith, Adam, 12
Smith-Hughes Act, 86–87, 101
South Carolina, 63
Sparsity, 42
Special aid funds, 40–43
Staff size, 21–22
State school support, 77–80, 83–84 (*see also* Revenue)
Stimulative grants, 40–41, 101, 107
Strayer, George D., Jr., 41, 52
Supplementary Educational Centers and Services, 98–99
Supreme Court, 53, 55–56
Surplus Revenue Deposit Act of 1836, 80

Survey of Current Business, 9n
Swearingen, Eugene L., 13

T

Tangible personal property, 60 (*see also* Property)
Tax leeway, 36–37, 44, 48
Tax rate, establishment of, 67–70
Tax relief, 50–51
Tax sharing, 59–60
Tax-shifting, 51
Tax sources (*figure*), 5 (*table*), 31, 58–60, 77–80, 83–84 (*see also* Revenue)
Teachers College Record, 55n
Teachers' salaries, 8, 22–23, 25
Teacher shortage, 8, 103
Texas, 81, 86
Transportation of pupils, 42, 53
Tuition income, 58–59

U

Underassessment, 62–66
Urban assistance, 42–43
U.S. Office of Education, 2n, 6, 88, 91, 94–95, 97, 99, 102

V

Values, school expenditure related to, 10–11
Vermont, 86
Vocational Education Act of 1963, 87–88, 94

W

Walker, Mabel, 63, 65
Weighted pupil, 20, 42
West Virginia, 86
Wisconsin, 50
Works Progress Administration, 89
World War I, 87
World War II, 91

Y

Youth Conservation Corps, 90